1987

LIVING HIGH

LIVING HIGH
Daily Marijuana Use Among Adults

Herbert Hendin, M.D.
Ann Pollinger Haas, Ph.D.
Paul Singer, M.D.
Melvyn Ellner, Ph.D.
Richard Ulman, Ph.D.

Center for Psychosocial Studies, N.Y., N.Y.

HUMAN SCIENCES PRESS, INC.
72 FIFTH AVENUE
NEW YORK, N.Y. 10011-8004

Printed in the United States of America
987654321

Library of Congress Cataloging-in-Publication Data

Living high.

  Bibliography: p.
  Includes index.
  1. Marihuana. 2. Drug abuse surveys—United States.
I. Hendin, Herbert. [DNLM: 1. Cannabis Abuse—in
adulthood. 2. Cannabis Abuse—psychology. 3. Social
Adjustment. WM 276 L785]
  HV5822.M3L58   1987   362.2   86-27634
  ISBN 0-89885-329-X

AUTHORS' AFFILIATIONS

Herbert Hendin, M.D., Director, Center for Psychosocial Studies; Professor of Psychiatry, New York Medical College; Director, Adult Psychiatric Outpatient Department, Metropolitan Hospital Center, New York, N.Y.

Ann Pollinger Haas, Ph.D., Associate Director, Center for Psychosocial Studies; Associate Professor of Health Services, Herbert H. Lehman College of the City University of New York; Research Associate Professor of Psychiatry, New York Medical College

Paul Singer, M.D., Associate Director, Center for Psychosocial Studies; Professor of Clinical Psychiatry, New York Medical College; Director of Psychiatry and Director of Psychiatric Residency Training, Metropolitan Hospital Center, New York, N.Y.

Melvyn Ellner, Ph.D., Research Associate, Center for Psychosocial Studies.

Richard Ulman, Ph.D., Research Associate, Center for Psychosocial Studies; Research Associate Professor of Psychiatry, New York Medical College; Consultant, Department of Psychiatry, Veterans Administration Hospital, Montrose, N.Y.

126,264

CONTENTS

ACKNOWLEDGEMENTS

This study of daily, long-term marijuana use among adults was supported by Grant No. DA-02730 from the National Institute on Drug Abuse. Meyer Glantz, Robert Battjes, and Barry Brown of the Institute reviewed the data with us and advised us on its analysis and presentation.

Arthur C. Carr, in addition to serving as a consultant in the analysis of the psychological tests, helped us in integrating the psychological and clinical data.

Ms. Margaret Williams patiently and carefully typed the many revisions of the text.

CHAPTER 1

BACKGROUND

The work that we will be describing was undertaken in order to explore the use of marijuana by adults who smoke daily and heavily, who have done so for many years, and who, at least in the several years prior to our study, have not used other drugs on a regular basis. We wished, in particular, to examine the adaptation of adults who, despite heavy marijuana use, appear, at least outwardly, to be leading productive lives. Our goal has been to obtain psychological understanding of the adaptive significance and consequences of long-term daily marijuana usage.

With few exceptions, the information that forms the basis of contemporary knowledge of marijuana use has been derived from studies of high school and college-age youngsters. Since it was the growing acceptance and use of marijuana by large numbers of middle-class young people, starting in the mid-1960s, that gave rise to social concern about marijuana, it is understandable that this population became the primary focus of research interest.

Survey results reported through the last decade have indicated steady increases in the number of young adults eighteen to twenty-five who have tried the drug, reaching a total of 68 percent by 1979, with 35 percent identified as current users (Petersen, 1980). Such statistics largely served to conceal, however, the more important aspect of the marijuana-smoking phenomenon: the number of young people who were using the drug to the extent that it was significantly interfering with their lives. Comparably, knowing the number of youngsters who have experimented with alcohol or tobacco is clearly less meaningful than identifying and understanding those who have become, or seem likely to become, problem drinkers or heavy smokers.

Most past studies of marijuana usage have included large percentages of subjects who use the drug minimally or only occasionally and others who use it as a part of a more general pattern of multidrug abuse. A primary focus of such research has been on the behavioral patterns seen among marijuana users, particularly those related to peer relationships, or on the psychological states that appear to characterize this population.

In a wide-ranging span of studies marijuana usage by young people has been correlated with such diverse variables as peer pressure and proximity to marijuana-smoking friends (Jessor, 1976; Jessor & Jessor, 1977; Jessor, Jessor, & Finney, 1973; Kandel, 1973; Kandel, Kessler, & Margulies, 1978); values and behaviors reflective of a "youth culture" life-style (Grinspoon, 1971; Hochman & Brill, 1973); poor academic performance, precocious sexual activity, and antisocial behavior (Jessor, Chase, & Donovan, 1980); feelings of hostility and aggression (Allen & West, 1968); anxiety, depression, and a lack of self-control (Kupfer, Detre, Korall, & Fajans, 1973); low self-esteem (Kaplan 1975a, 1975b; 1978; Norem-Hebeisen, 1975); difficulties in establishing meaningful relationships with others (Esman, 1967; Mirin, Shapiro, Meyer, Pillard, & Fisher, 1971); and "amotivational" personality characteristics (McGlothin & West, 1968; Kolansky & Moore, 1971, 1972; Kornhaber, 1971; Kolodny, Masters, Kolodner, & Toro, 1974; Maugh, 1974). Such correlations, however, have not contributed to an understanding of the meaning for marijuana-smoking youngsters of their behavior or of the underlying motivations for marijuana usage. Moreover, the correlations, once established, have tended to divert attention to misdirected questions as to which came first, the marijuana smoking or the correlate.

In our past investigations of drug use among young people we have found that using intensive, unstructured interviewing, rather than the much more widely employed self-report questionnaires or limited-contact interviews, makes it possible to see both the marijuana smoking and related behaviors in the context of the individual's total psychosocial adaptation. In the case of college youngsters who smoked marijuana exclusively and heavily (Hendin 1973, 1975, 1980), for example, we found that their drug behavior was not responsible in any direct or simple way for poor school performance, as some have maintained. Neither could it be considered a reaction to academic difficulties, nor an incidental concomitant of a change to a non-achievement-oriented life-style, as others have claimed. Rather, marijuana was seen as playing a characteristic, definable, defensive role in these students' attempts to deal with conflicts over competition and aggression. Further, in each of 15 heavy marijuana-smoking students who were intensively studied, adaptive difficulties were identified that appeared to derive in major part from troubled family relationships.

That study, which was part of a larger investigation of drug abuse among college students, indicated that those who use a specific type of drug fairly exclusively (e.g., heroin, amphetamines, psychedelics, etc.) provide an excellent source of information concerning the function of a particular drug in an individual's adaptation. In the case of marijuana-smoking youngsters the apparent connection of the drug behavior to long-standing difficulties within the family led us to a subsequent study focusing on marijuana-abusing adolescents who were still living at home (Hendin, Pollinger, Ulman, & Carr, 1981). In that research the subjects included not only the youngsters but also their parents and, in most cases, a non-marijuana-abusing sibling. In addition to a prolonged series of intensive interviews with all participants in each family, the marijuana abusers and their siblings were given a battery of psychological tests.

A primary goal of the study was to understand the family psychodynamics in the context of which a marijuana-abusing youngster as well as a close age-order sibling who did not abuse drugs had emerged. Several different patterns were observed across the families who were studied, even though in virtually every case we found that the marijuana abuser had received the worst rather than the best of what the parents had to offer. In some cases this occurred because the youngster was born after the family's emotional reserves had been drained by prior children. In such families the overall tensions as well as the individual problems intensified with each succeeding child. In other families, the marijuana-abusing youngster had long been seen as mirroring the parents' limitations, anxieties, and insecurities, whereas his sibling was regarded as having the parents' best characteristics. Each child tended to be treated accordingly. In some families the parents' exaggerated and rigid expectations of a favorite child, and their subsequent disappointment in that child, resulted in a shift in their affections to another of the siblings. In other families parental difficulties caused problems for a particular child when he or she was quite young, and even though the parents had resolved these difficulties the child's troubles persisted.

Through the study marijuana was found to have a variety of functions for adolescents: as a defiant or provocative act directed against parents in particular and by extension to other authority figures; as a self-destructive act; as a modifier of disturbing emotions, such as anger; as a reenforcer of fantasies of effortless, grandiose success; and as a help in withdrawing from conflicts concerning competition and achievement.

In all of its functions marijuana served to detach these adolescents from the problems of the real world—from their anger and unhappiness with their parents and from the need to work and compete to achieve success. In so doing, it permitted some to appear casual or lighthearted while inside they felt miserable. Fantasies of being destined for a special fate, to become rich without work, and to excel at a sport they scarcely played were typical of the parody of success, achievement, and confidence that marijuana sustained in some of the young men. The young female marijuana abusers, although not usually expecting particular greatness, nevertheless maintained a magical belief that good things would happen to them: college acceptance while flunking out of high school or happiness in love while dating unresponsive or abusive young men. For all of these adolescents, marijuana helped sustain in an unrealistic way the desire for power, control, achievement, and emotional fullness.

Although marijuana abuse was found to span a spectrum of needs for the individuals involved, all of its functions were related in the abusers' attempts to deal with long-standing feelings of being deprived of approval or acceptance within their families. The abusers' belief that nothing they could do would make them loved members of their families served to produce or intensify a retreat from competitive achievement and to turn them toward methods of passive consolation in which grandiose dreams of love or success could be sustained.

The psychological tests did not indicate significant differences between the marijuana abusers and the non-drug-abusing siblings. Rather, they consistently showed that both groups of youngsters had comparable difficulty in dealing with unstructured situations. The interview material, however, suggested that the non-drug-abusers knew how to avoid putting themselves in such situations; their avoidance of drugs was partly related to their desire to maintain control and structure in their lives. The ability to find, create, and operate in structured situations, whether at school or in personal relationships, was an important attribute these siblings had developed in their families and were able to use outside the family as well.

That study provided considerable evidence that the youngsters' overt expression of their psychopathology—whether in the form of destructive acting-out behavior, withdrawal, or rigid conformity to parental standards—could be accounted for by the family psychodynamics which permitted, directed, and maintained the way marijuana abusers and their siblings behaved. The adaptation of adolescents, however, is often highly fluid, and this applies to their drug use as well. Follow-up interviews with the youngsters who participated in the study, which continued for a period of four subsequent years, revealed marked changes in many. Particularly among those who moved away from their families, a number of positive outcomes were observed in the direction of diminished drug use and more stable social adaptations. Others, however, had become further entrenched in a drifting, aimless existence, including in some cases heavy use of cocaine or alcohol. For still others marijuana patterns begun during adolescence appeared to have become an established part of their daily routines, despite the changes that had occurred in their life circumstances.

These observations have raised many questions about the role of marijuana in the lives of adults who, although generally no longer enmeshed in the struggles with parents and siblings that characterized the adolescents we studied, are often coping with the pressures of jobs, relationships, marriage, and perhaps even children of their own. Within this context, what functions does daily heavy, marijuana smoking perform? Is the use of the drug to such an extent at all compatible with what this society regards as "normal" adult adaptation? Perhaps most basically, what are the long-term psychosocial consequences of heavy marijuana smoking for individuals whose use has spanned a period of many years, often reaching back to adolescence?

Although the prevalence of marijuana smoking generally appears to decrease among people over the age of twenty-five (Miller & Cissin, 1983; Clayton & Ritter, 1984), use of the drug has been predicted to be expanding into the older age groups (Hochman & Brill, 1973; Jessor, 1979; Richards, 1981). A review of the existing research literature has revealed a paucity of studies, however, focusing specifically on the regular, heavy adult user. What information has been reported about marijuana smoking among persons over the age of twenty-one has been disproportionately derived from minorities in the lower socioeconomic classes (Robins, Dervish, & Murphy, 1970) or from specialized occupational groups such as professional musicians (Winick, 1970), with limited potential to illuminate understanding of the behavior among the general adult population.

One notable exception is an analysis of marijuana use among white, middle-class adults by McGlothlin and his colleagues at the University of California (McGlothlin, Arnold, & Rowan, 1970) that was undertaken as part of a larger study of the effects of LSD. From among a large pool of subjects who had volunteered to take LSD under experimental conditions, 29 individuals (22 men and 7 women) were identified as having at some time used marijuana two or more times a week for a minimum of two years. Thirteen persons in this subgroup were working in arts-related professions. Only 14 of the 29 were currently using marijuana regularly, and only 6 on a daily basis.

In interviews with this subsample, the most frequently cited reasons for using marijuana were to produce a "high" or euphoria, to relax, to enhance creative productivity, and to relieve tension or stress. Other reasons somewhat less frequently given included the desire to increase sexual satisfaction, relieve depression, increase sociability, and cope with uncomfortable situations.

Less than one-third of the group saw marijuana as having any long-term effects; however, among those reporting positive effects, increased self-insight, tolerance, creativity, spontaneity, and sexual freedom were most frequently mentioned. Negative effects, identified by only two individuals, included lung irritation, absentmindedness, and reduced discipline and productivity.

In exploring other life-style, personality, and attitudinal characteristics, the marijuana users were found to exhibit relatively unstructured and unstable patterns in both work and relationships, and a proneness toward non-drug-induced regressive states as measured by a hypnotic susceptibility test. They also were found to have a much higher than normal belief in the validity of such paranormal phenomena as astrology and ESP.

Although the findings provided some initial insight into an area about which little had previously been known, the authors of this study conceded that the generalizability of those findings was limited by the fact that the sample was taken from among individuals willing to take LSD experimentally, many of whom were already frequent LSD users. In addition, although levels of marijuana use were relatively low overall, 79 percent of those studied had a history of heavy alcohol use, and 66 percent were frequent, regular users of stimulants, particularly amphetamines. Even more fundamentally, the study's reliance on a single-interview, self-report procedure, like so many past investigations of marijuana use among adolescents, precluded an understanding of both the drug-taking and related behaviors in the context of the individual's total psychosocial adaptation.

Another more recent study by Halikas and his colleagues

(1983) has pointed to the complexity involved in attempting to assess the role of marijuana in the lives of adult users. Their analysis, which used multivariate strategies in attempting to determine the impact of frequent marijuana use on negative social functioning, clearly established the importance of examining the drug behavior within the framework of a much wider range of psychosocial variables, including ones related to childhood history. Also underscored by this study, however, was the limitation of quantitative analyses in providing an understanding of why some individuals turn to heavy marijuana use and what impact that has on their psychosocial functioning.

The present study has been undertaken in order to fill the important gap in our knowledge of the psychodynamic functions and consequences of long-term, chronic use by adults. Specifically, we wished to examine in detail the adaptation of long-term daily marijuana users who appeared to be currently making a satisfactory social adjustment and who were not referred for problems related to their use of marijuana.

CHAPTER 2

RATIONALE AND DESIGN
OF THE STUDY

Consistent with the study's primary aim of understanding the psychodynamic functions of daily, heavy marijuana use among adult long-term users, a methodological approach was sought that would allow this behavior to be explored individually and intensively while providing insight into its occurrence within the widest possible range of adult users. Based on our earlier work with adolescents (Hendin, Pollinger, Ulman, & Carr, 1981) we felt that more could be learned about the psychodynamics of marijuana use through intensively studying a small, carefully selected group of heavy long-term users for whom marijuana was their only currently used drug than through the more commonly employed survey-type design focusing on large numbers of users of varying amounts of marijuana, often in conjunction with other drugs.

The paucity of existing research data that could serve to guide the selection of an appropriate group of long-term, heavy marijuana-smoking adults pointed to the need to first gather a systematic data base on this general population. Thus, the initial method used in the study was a survey that sought to obtain basic information on demographic, socioeconomic, social, and psychological characteristics of daily heavy marijuana smokers, which in turn could be used to identify and select various types of users for in-depth study.

Over the course of a 1-year period, advertisements were placed in general- and special-interest magazines, journals, and newspapers that circulate throughout the urban and suburban areas of the New York metropolitan region. These included such diverse publications as *New York* magazine, *The New York Review of Books*, *The Village Voice*, *Pennsysaver*, and *The Chief* (civil service trade journal). Each advertisement contained essentially the same message: that people over the age of nineteen who had been heavy marijuana smokers for at least the past 2 years were being sought for a research project, that all information would be strictly confidential, and that they would be paid for their participation. Both a telephone number and a mailing address were provided for respondents to use in requesting additional information and an application form.

As inquiries came in (more than 95 percent of which were by telephone), the procedures of the study were explained. Specifically, each person was told that at the present time we were interested in obtaining information through a brief interview and a written questionnaire from a large number of heavy marijuana-using adults and that their suitability for this phase of the study would be determined on the basis of the information they would provide on the application form. They were also told that the initial session, for those selected to participate, would last approximately 1 to 1½ hours, for which a $25 fee would be paid. Finally, it was mentioned that, based on the initial interviews and questionnaire data, a smaller number of individuals would be selected to participate in a more extensive phase of the study, requiring about 8 to 10 hours, for which an additional fee of $200 would be paid.

Individuals who were interested in applying for participation were asked to provide names and addresses so that an application form could be sent. In many cases this prompted questions about the researchers' affiliation with government officials and procedures regarding confidentially, but in all except a handful of cases, names and addresses were eventually provided. (A few of the least trusting came in person to pick up their application forms.)

Concurrent with the advertising process, personal contacts were made with individuals known to be heavy marijuana users, and copies of the one-page application form were given to them to circulate among others whom they knew to be heavy, long-term smokers. Additional forms also were given to those who completed the initial session and who indicated having appropriate friends, relatives, or co-workers who also might be interested in participating in the study.

Through these various procedures a total of 383 completed applications eventually were obtained, including 175 (46%) from white men, 116 (30%) from white women, 69 (18%) from black men, and 23 (6%) from black women. To eliminate the potentially confounding variable of race, it was decided that the focus of the study would be exclusively on whites, and 150 persons were selected in stages from among the 291 white applicants.

In making these selections attention was first given to the information the applicants provided on the form about the number of years they had been smoking, the number of days per week they currently smoked, and the times during the day when they typically smoked (i.e., mornings, lunchtime, after-work hours, evenings, bedtime). All of those selected indicated long-term use of marijuana, current use at a level of at least 6 days per week, and use during both daytime and evening or night-time hours. The variables of sex, education, and occupation were then considered in order to create the broadest possible range of participants.

In a telephone conversation with each individual selected, the information provided on the application was confirmed and use of drugs other than marijuana was questioned. Those with current heavy use of any other drugs, including alcohol, were eliminated from consideration; others were scheduled for screening sessions and the questionnaire.

At the outset of the screening session subjects were asked to tell the interviewer something about themselves and their present life. This brief (5–10-minute) introductory portion of the interview typically elicited basic information about current job and living situation, marital status, and family background.

Following this introduction the interviewer moved to the topic of marijuana and, using a set of structured questions, explored in detail the subject's history and current patterns of use.

Specific attention was directed toward determining the exact amount of marijuana smoked, and a variety of questions about the number of marijuana cigarettes smoked per day, the number of ounces of marijuana used per month, and so on were included as a measure of internal validity of the subject's responses. A number of additional questions sought specific information about where, when, and with whom the subject used marijuana, as well as his history of the use of drugs other than marijuana.

Subjects were then given a 43-page questionnaire that they completed in a private room. The majority of the questions on this instrument were cooperatively developed by several groups and individuals throughout the country (including ourselves) who were conducting research into marijuana use with support from the National Institute on Drug Abuse (Huba, Bentler, & Newcomb, 1981). The questionnaire as developed by the group included an initial section covering reasons for smoking marijuana, perceptions of its short- and long-term effects, and negative reactions to marijuana that had been experienced. The second section focused on the individual's physical status, health problems, and health-related behavior. (Although each of our subjects completed this section of the questionnaire along with the others, this area was not a primary focus of our study and is not included in the present analysis.) The third section explored such general social and psychological dimensions as illegal and antisocial behavior, patterns of social interaction, life satisfaction, self-esteem, and psychological problems and complaints.

Our questionnaire also included two additional sections: one contained items dealing with family background and general biographical material, and the other was a Psychological Data Sheet (Carr, 1972) that elicited more information about the subject's relationships, sense of self, and general psychological status. Questions in all except the last section were close-ended, and the entire questionnaire took most subjects approximately one hour to complete.

Once they had completed the questionnaire, subjects were asked about their willingness to participate in the second phase of the study, providing they were selected. All subjects who completed the screening interview and questionnaire agreed to further participation.

On a regular weekly basis those who were conducting the initial interviews presented an overview of each subject to the full research staff, who collectively reviewed the interviewer's notes and the subject's questionnaire material. On the basis of these discussions subjects were selected for participation in the second stage of the study. In making these selections persons were sought who were representative of a unique type of marijuana smoker seen among the larger group, insofar as they were characterized by particular constellations of demographic, socioeconomic, social, and psychological variables. Rather than reflecting the larger group in a rigidly statistical way, however, individuals were chosen because of their potential to illuminate certain patterns of daily heavy marijuana usage that had not previously been explored.

A total of 15 cases—eight men and seven women—ultimately were selected from among the 150 heavy marijuana users who completed the screening session and questionnaire. In the second phase of the research each of these individuals participated in a series of five relatively unstructured interviews that explored in depth their current lives, including work, relationships, values and goals; family backgrounds, childhood, and adolescent histories; past and current history of marijuana use; and the interrelationships among all of these variables. Each of the interviews with a particular case was conducted by the same member of the research staff and sessions were scheduled at intervals of between two and five days apart. Sessions lasted between 60 and 75 minutes and were tape recorded for later transcription. In addition, the interviewer wrote a detailed process note following each session in which were recorded the salient issues discussed during the interview, clinical impressions, and areas to be explored in the subsequent interviews.

Approximately midway through the series of interviews the person was scheduled to see the project psychologist for a battery of psychological tests. During one session, usually lasting 3 to 3½ hours, the Weschler Adult Intelligence Scale-Revised (WAIS-R), the Draw-A-Person Test, and the Rorschach Test were administered. At the close of the session the individual was given the Minnesota Multiphasic Personality Inventory (MMPI) to complete at home and return at his next scheduled interview.

During the fifth interview subjects were encouraged to ask

any questions they wished about the interviews. The content, extent, and depth of the interviewer's response was geared to the person's desire for and ability to integrate such information; subsequent sessions also were offered in order to discuss further issues that had come up in the interviews or psychological tests. Each subject was then told that additional interviews might be required, for which he would be reimbursed at a rate of $25 per session, and that he wold be contacted if this became necessary. Following completion of the fifth interview, subjects were paid the $200 fee.

During the last four months of the study—an average of 20 months after completing the initial series of interviews—each individual was recontacted for follow-up, and each was seen two, three, or four times depending on what had transpired in the individual's life in the interim and how this related to his use of marijuana.

Once all the data had been collected on a particular case, typed transcripts of each interview session were independently reviewed by at least two clinically trained members of the research staff in order to identify the functions that chronic heavy marijuana appeared to perform for the individual and to obtain an understanding of how this fit into his overall psychosocial functioning. Findings of the reviewers were presented in both written and oral forms to the entire research staff, with the goal of resolving any inconsistencies in interpretation that existed between the reviewers. Wherever necessary, additional interview sessions with the subject were held to clarify points or obtain additional information. Following the final meeting on each case the interviewer compiled all findings into a comprehensive case summary.

The data obtained through the psychological tests were analyzed independently. The MMPI was computer scored and interpreted by Roche Research Services. Following scoring by the project psychologist, the results of the WAIS-R and the Rorschach also were subjected to computer analysis (using the services of Leon Morris and Century Diagnostics, respectively). With regard to the Rorschach analysis, emphasis was placed on those aspects of the individual's protocol that were deemed "highly significant" based on the calculation of score ratios that have been found through prior research to be both valid and reliable; i.e., test results that were approximately two times greater or lesser than the normal value. The computer analyses for both the WAIS-R and the Rorschach also were reviewed and validated by Dr. Arthur C. Carr, a clinical psychologist and a recognized authority on those two tests (1980, 1984) who served as a project consultant. A second consultant, Dr. Emmanuel Hammer, lent his considerable expertise with the Draw-A-Person Test (1980) in blind interpretations of all drawings provided by the subjects on this measure.

Once all material had been written up on a case, several meetings were held for the purpose of reviewing the summary reports. The emphasis in these meetings was on identifying areas of agreement and inconsistency between the clinical and psychological data, and identifying a final set of psychological and psychodynamic functions of daily, heavy marijuana use for that individual.

In the next chapter a summary is presented of the data that were obtained through the initial screening interviews with the 150 heavy marijuana-smoking adults who participated in the study and the questionnaires they completed. This is followed in Chapter 4 by a series of reports on six of the cases that were studied intensively, each of which includes a synopsis of the questionnaire data, the material obtained through the semi-structured interviews, the psychological test results, and an integrating case summary.

These cases are followed by Chapter 5, which presents the key findings of the study. The first section of that chapter addresses the primary question that guided the study, focusing on the functions of long-term, heavy marijuana use among adults. Next, those findings are discussed, with special emphasis on contrasting the significance of heavy marijuana use in the overall adaptation of adults with what we had learned from our earlier studies of adolescents. The third section contains a discussion of what was learned through this study concerning methodological issues in drug research, focusing on an evaluation of our approach, which featured the combined use of a written questionnaire, psychodynamic interviews, and psychological tests. The volume concludes with a brief summation of our findings regarding adults who are daily users of marijuana.

CHAPTER 3

A PSYCHOSOCIAL OVERVIEW OF DAILY MARIJUANA-USING ADULTS

In this chapter we present a summary of the data obtained from the 150 heavy marijuana-smoking adults who, responding to newspaper and magazine advertisements, volunteered to complete the initial interview and written questionnaire. The chapter is divided into four sections, the first of which provides a general demographic picture of the complete group. This is followed by a brief description of the family backgrounds of the individuals whom we studied. The third section presents detailed information about the patterns of marijuana use seen among them, and the final section contains an overview of findings related to various social and psychological dimensions of their lives.

DEMOGRAPHIC PROFILE

The 150 subjects studied included 99 men (66%) and 51 women (34%) ranging in age from twenty to fifty-six, with an average age of approximately thirty-one years. As shown in Table 1, which presents the distribution of subjects by sex and age,

Table 1. Distribution of Subjects by Sex and Age

Age group	Male N	Male %	Female N	Female %	Total N	Total %
20–24	11	11.1	9	17.6	20	13.3
25–29	32	32.3	18	35.3	50	33.3
30–34	28	28.3	14	27.5	42	28.0
35–39	18	18.2	6	11.8	24	16.0
40–44	8	8.1	3	5.9	11	7.3
45 and over	2	2.0	1	2.0	3	2.0
Total	99	100.0	51	100.0	150	100.0

the frequencies of men and women in each of the age groups roughly paralleled the proportion of each sex in the total group. Overall, the women we studied were slightly younger than the men.

All of the subjects were Caucasian. Slightly more than 95 percent were American-born, with more than 70 percent coming from the northeastern United States. All were U.S. citizens and had spent most of their childhood, adolescence, and adult years in this country.

Although almost 90 percent of the subjects indicated having been raised in a particular religion (see Family Background section below), Table 2 shows that almost half of the group (48%) did not currently express a preference for any religion. Less than one-fifth currently identified themselves as Jewish, 16 percent were Catholic, and approximately 5 percent were Protestant. Fourteen percent described themselves as being affiliated. with a non-denominational group or an Eastern religion.

Approximately half of the total group indicated that they regarded religion as "not important" in terms of their current lives. Only 18 percent described religion as having significant importance in their lives, and only approximately 6 percent indicated regular attendance at religious services.

The data in Table 3, which presents the distribution of the total group by sex and current marital status, show that the ma-

Table 2. Distribution of Subjects by Sex and Current Religious Preference

Religious preference	Male		Female		Total	
	N	%	N	%	N	%
Jewish	16	16.2	10	19.6	26	17.3
Catholic	18	18.1	6	11.7	24	16.0
Protestant	6	6.1	1	2.0	7	4.7
Other	16	16.2	5	9.8	21	14.0
None	43	43.4	29	56.9	72	48.0
Total	99	100.0	51	100.0	150	100.0

jority of the subjects studied (60%) were single at the time of their interviews. The next highest subgroup (22%) consisted of those who were married and living with their spouses at the time of the study. Of the 116 subjects who were divorced, separated, or single, 22 were living with an unmarried partner and another 44 were involved in a steady relationship with another individual. Only 32 individuals, or 21 percent, had children, whereas 118, or 78 percent, did not. Among those who had children, all but two of the subjects lived with their children at least most of the time.

As can be seen in Tables 4 and 5, almost 75 percent of the group had at least some college education at the time they were

Table 3. Distribution of Subjects by Sex and Current Marital Status

Marital status	Male		Female		Total	
	N	%	N	%	N	%
Married	25	25.3	9	17.6	34	22.7
Divorced	11	11.1	7	13.8	18	12.0
Separated	6	6.1	2	3.9	8	5.3
Single	57	57.5	33	64.7	90	60.0
Total	99	100.0	51	100.0	150	100.0

**Table 4. Distribution of Subjects by Sex
and Educational Level**

Educational level	Male		Female		Total	
	N	%	N	%	N	%
Some high school	7	7.1	3	5.9	10	6.7
High school diploma	18	18.2	13	25.5	31	20.7
Some college	36	36.3	21	41.2	57	38.0
College degree	28	28.3	12	23.5	40	26.7
Some graduate school	6	6.1	2	3.9	8	5.3
Graduate degree	4	4.0	0	0.0	4	2.6
Total	99	100.0	51	100.0	150	100.0

initially seen, and approximately one-third had a college degree. Relatively little variation in educational levels was noted between the men and the women or among the different age groups included in the research.

More than eight of ten subjects were employed at least part-time at the time of the study, with the rate of employment among the men (87%) only slightly higher than among the women (84%). The occupations of the employed and unemployed cut across a wide range of professional, white-collar, and blue-collar areas, as can be seen in Tables 6 and 7.

The individual income for the 150 subjects studied during the year immediately preceding their interviews ranged from zero to $100,000, with an average annual income for the group of $16,867. As shown in Table 8, men were somewhat more likely than women to be in the upper income groups.

When combined income was considered for the 62 individuals in the sample who indicated that they pooled their financial resources with a spouse or partner, a somewhat higher socioeconomic picture emerged. Among this subgroup, combined income ranged from a low of $6,000 to a high of $185,000, with an average of approximately $34,000.

Table 5. Distribution of Subjects by Age and Educational Level

Educational level	Age						Total	
	20–24	25–29	30–34	35–39	40–44	45+	N	%
Some high school	—	5	3	—	1	1	10	6.7
High school diploma	4	14	6	4	2	1	31	20.7
Some college	9	10	17	17	4	1	57	38.0
College degree	5	18	13	2	2	1	40	26.7
Some graduate school	2	2	2	1	1		8	5.3
Graduate degree	—	1	1	—	1	1	4	2.7
Total	20	50	42	24	11	3	150	100.0

Table 6. Distribution of Subjects by Sex and Type of Occupation

Type of occupation	Male		Female		Total	
	N	%	N	%	N	%
Professional	14	14.1	5	9.8	19	12.7
White-collar	41	41.5	29	56.9	70	46.6
Blue-collar	22	22.2	4	7.8	26	17.3
Arts-related	19	19.2	11	21.6	30	20.0
Other	3	3.0	2	3.9	5	3.4
Total	99	100.0	51	100.0	150	100.0

Table 7. Distribution of Subjects by Sex and Exact Occupation

Occupation	Male	Female	Total
Professional			
Accountant (CPA)	2		2
Architect	1		1
Attorney	2		2
Computer programmer	2		2
Nurse		1	1
Occupational therapist		1	1
Psychologist (psychotherapist)	1		1
Publisher	1		1
Statistician	1	1	2
Social worker	1		1
Teacher	1	2	3
Unemployed professional	2		2
Total Professional	14	5	19
White Collar			
Administrative assistant	1		1
Advertising account representative		1	1

Table 7. Continued.

Occupation	Male	Female	Total
Advertising copywriter	1		1
Assistant sales manager (retail)	1		1
Assistant service manager (automotive)	1		1
Assistant news editor	1		1
Business management assistant	3	1	4
Child care worker		1	1
Civil service supervisor	1		1
Customer service rep		1	1
General office, clerical	6	8	14
Manager, retail store		1	1
Medical aide/technician	3	2	5
Medical health insurance coordinator		1	1
Nursing school assistant administrator		1	1
Owner, small business	2		2
Paralegal	2	1	3
Patient coordinator		1	1
Personnel manager	1	1	2
Project administrator		1	1
Real estate broker	1		1
Research assistant	2		2
Research technician	1		1
Salesperson	8	1	9
Stockbroker assistant	2		2
Wholesale distributor	2		2
Unemployed white collar (including housewives)	2	7	9
Total White Collar	41	29	70
Blue Collar			
Bartender	2		2
Cook	1	1	2

Table 7. Continued.

Occupation	Male	Female	Total
Driver, bus	2		2
Driver, truck	2		2
Driver, taxi	2		2
Landscaper	1		1
Mechanic	1		1
Skilled tradesperson	3		3
Telephone installer	1		1
Unskilled tradesperson	2		2
Waitress		3	3
Unemployed blue collar	5		5
Total Blue Collar	22	· 4	26

Arts-Related			
Actor/actress	1	1	2
Artist	4	3	7
Art instructor	1	2	3
Craftsmaker		1	1
Filmmaker	1	1	2
Manager, recording studio	1		1
Mapmaker	1		1
Musician	2		2
Photographer	1		1
Production assistant (TV)	1		1
Screen writer	1		1
Writer	4	3	7
Unemployed, arts	1		1
Total Arts-Related	19	11	30

Other			
Graduate student	1	1	2
Unemployed, no established occupation	2	1	3
Total Other	3	2	5

**Table 8. Distribution of Subjects by Sex
and Individual Annual Income**

Annual income (in thousands)	Male		Female		Total	
	N	%	N	%	N	%
0–10	33	33.3	26	60.0	59	39.3
11–20	40	40.4	19	37.3	59	39.3
21–30	13	13.1	1	1.9	14	9.3
31–50	9	9.1	5	9.8	14	9.3
51 and over	4	4.1	0	0.0	4	2.7
Total	99	100.0	51	100.0	150	100.0

FAMILY BACKGROUND

More than three-quarters of those we studied lived with both parents for all or almost all of the time they were growing up. Eight percent lived with their mothers only and approximately 10 percent lived with one parent (in most cases the mother) and other relatives. Only 4 percent of the subjects did not live with at least one parent for most of the time while growing up. As a group the subjects had an approximate average of two siblings, with 7 percent having no siblings and 32 percent having three or more.

Eighteen subjects, representing 12 percent of the total group, experienced the death of their fathers before they were nineteen years old, and 19, or 13 percent, had a mother die before they were that age. Twenty-one subjects, or 14 percent, reported that their parents had divorced before they reached nineteen.

Table 9 shows the distribution of the subjects by the religion in which they were raised. Although almost nine of ten described themselves as having been raised in a particular religion, only 14 percent said they had come from homes in which at least one parent was "very religious."

In 75 percent of the families the father was described as the

Table 9. Distribution of Subjects by Religion in Which They Were Raised

Religion in which raised	N	%
Jewish	42	28.0
Catholic	60	40.0
Protestant	26	17.3
Other	6	4.0
None	16	10.7
Total	150	100.0

main wage earner, although 66 percent of the subjects said their mothers had worked at least some of the time while they were growing up. As can be seen in Table 10, the largest proportion of both fathers and mothers held white collar positions.

Among all 150 subjects, the average family income during the period in which they were in high school was approximately $14,000, with 40 percent of the families earning less than $15,000, 30 percent earning between $15,000 and $25,000, and 30 percent earning more than $25,000.

More than two-fifths of the total group (42%) described their family relationships as having been generally very close during the period they were growing up. An almost equal proportion (44%) indicated that family members had generally kept

Table 10. Distribution of Subjects' Parents by Type of Occupation

Type of occupation	Father		Mother	
	N	%	N	%
Professional	38	25.4	18	12.0
White-collar	60	40.0	62	41.3
Blue-collar	45	30.0	14	9.3
Arts-related	5	3.3	5	3.3
Not employed	2	1.3	51	34.1
Total	150	100.0	150	100.0

to themselves, and the remaining subgroup (14%) described their relationships with particular family members as having been close whereas with others there was considerable distance. In describing particular problems that had characterized their families while they were growing up, 32 percent of the subjects indicated that their fathers had had a serious physical illness, and 27 percent said their mothers had been seriously ill. Almost 14 percent of fathers and 21 percent of mothers were described as having had an emotional illness at some point during the subject's childhood or adolescence. Almost 20 percent of the subjects indicated that their fathers had had problems with drinking, and 7 percent characterized their fathers as having been regular users of drugs. Mothers' alcohol-related problems were identified by 15 percent of the group, and 20 percent said their mothers had been regular drug users. Only about 4 percent indicated that their fathers had had any difficulties with the law, however, and fewer than 1 percent described their mothers as having had such problems.

Overall, these individuals described themselves as having been quite active socially while growing up, with almost half having participated in three or more clubs or long-term activities during childhood and adolescence. A majority (55%), however, described themselves as having had "just a few" close friends, with approximately one-third (34%) indicating having had "lots" of close friends and the rest (11%) saying that they had had "hardly any."

The majority of the subject group (58%) had generally done well in school, whereas only 13% said they had not done well overall. More than half (56%), however, described themselves as having been indifferent to or having disliked school; 28 percent cut school frequently, and 12 percent had dropped out of high school.

In response to an open-ended questionnaire item asking the subjects about particular difficulties they might have experienced while growing up, more than one-third of the group (39%) identified no such difficulties. About half of the subjects (53%) responded that they had had difficulties of a fairly minor nature. Most frequently mentioned among this subgroup were frightening nightmares, fears of separation from home and

Table 11.   Distribution of Subjects by Sex and
Age of First Marijuana Use

Age of first use	Male		Female		Total	
	N	%	N	%	N	%
11 or younger	6	6.1	1	2.0	7	4.7
12–14	27	27.3	15	29.4	42	28.8
15–17	33	33.3	22	43.1	55	36.7
18–21	21	21.2	8	15.7	29	19.3
22–25	11	11.1	4	7.8	15	10.0
26 and older	1	1.0	1	2.0	2	1.3
Total	99	100.0	51	100.0	150	100.0

family, shyness, temper tantrums, bed-wetting, difficulties making friends, being overweight, school-related problems, and persistent illnesses. The remaining 8 percent of the subjects identified problems of a more serious nature, including physical abuse by parents, pervasive school phobia, and serious behavioral or emotional problems.

MARIJUANA PATTERNS

On the average the 150 subjects in the study first used marijuana at the age of sixteen. As shown in Table 11, men and women showed very similar distributions across the various age groups in which marijuana use first began.

Two to five years after first using marijuana all 150 subjects had begun regular daily or almost daily use (see Table 12). The average age for beginning such regular use among the group was about twenty.

At the time the subjects were interviewed almost 93 percent had been smoking marijuana on a daily basis for at least three years, and almost one-third of the group had been daily smokers for a period of ten years or more. As can be seen in Table 13, approximately three-quarters had smoked at least 3,000 times, and almost half had smoked more than 7,000 times. All subjects had

**Table 12. Distribution of Subjects by Sex and Age of
Beginning Regular Daily Use of Marijuana**

Age of beginning regular use	Male		Female		Total	
	N	%	N	%	N	%
12–14	9	9.1	3	5.9	12	8.0
15–17	21	21.2	13	25.6	34	22.7
18–21	38	38.4	19	37.3	57	38.0
22–25	20	20.2	8	15.7	28	18.7
26–30	9	9.1	4	7.8	13	8.6
31 and older	2	2.0	4	7.8	6	4.0
Total	99	100.0	51	100.0	150	100.0

smoked on a daily basis for at least one year prior to being seen, and the large majority (70%) said that they would find it hard to get through an entire week without smoking marijuana. As a group the subjects consumed an average of slightly under two ounces of marijuana per month, with an average equivalent of almost 3½ marijuana cigarettes per day.

Almost half of the subjects (47%) expressed satisfaction with the amount they were currently smoking, whereas only 4 percent indicated that they would like to be smoking more. More than one-third (37%) said they wanted to cut down the amount

**Table 13. Distribution of Subjects by Sex and Total
Number of Times Smoking Marijuana**

Number of times smoking marijuana	Male		Female		Total	
	N	%	N	%	N	%
1,000–3,000	25	25.3	13	25.5	38	25.4
3,001–5,000	19	19.2	10	19.6	29	19.3
5,001–7,000	9	9.0	7	13.7	16	10.7
7,001 or more	46	46.5	21	41.2	67	44.7
Total	99	100.0	51	100.0	150	100.0

**Table 14. Distribution of Subjects by Sex and Feelings
about Current Level of Use of Marijuana**

	Male		Female		Total	
Feelings about use	*N*	*%*	*N*	*%*	*N*	*%*
Would like to smoke more	4	4.0	2	3.9	6	4.0
Satisfied with present amount	45	45.5	25	49.0	70	46.7
Would like to cut down	38	38.4	18	35.3	56	37.3
Would like to stop	12	12.1	6	11.8	18	12.0
Total	99	100.0	51	100.0	150	100.0

they were currently smoking, and the remaining 12 percent expressed the desire to stop altogether. Similar proportions of men and women were found in each of these categories, as can be seen in Table 14.

During the one-month period immediately prior to being interviewed the subjects had spent an average of $81 on marijuana. Although in almost every case the primary source of the money spent on marijuana was the subject's own income, almost 6 of every ten indicated that they regularly or occasionally sold marijuana in order to reduce the cost of their own supply.

About half of the group were also regular tobacco smokers, averaging over one pack of cigarettes per day. A little more than one-quarter described themselves as regular users of beer, and about 17 percent indicated regular consumption of either wine or hard liquor. Most had tried a wide variety of other drugs, and approximately 5 percent had past regular use of heroin and other narcotics. In keeping with the selection criteria used in the study, very few were currently regular users of any drug other than marijuana, with the exception of 9 percent who used cocaine on a regular basis, 7 percent who used hashish, and 5 percent who used Quaaludes. Occasional use of hashish was indicated by 60 percent; 51 percent used cocaine occasionally, and 22 percent had occasional use of Quaaludes.

In response to questions about where they used marijuana, almost three-quarters of the subjects (73%) said they felt an experienced user could smoke it in virtually any context. Certain variations were apparent, however, in regard to where the subjects smoked most frequently. More than two-thirds of the group (68%) said that most of the time when they smoked they were at home, and another 9 percent responded that home was the only place that they used marijuana.

The total group was evenly divided among those who smoked marijuana while at work at least some of the time, those who smoked at work only occasionally, and those who never smoked at work. The large majority (75%), however, said that much of their social life took place while they were smoking marijuana. Friends' homes were identified by 82 percent as a regular place in which they smoked, and parties were mentioned by 87 percent. A large number (73%) said they regularly smoked while driving in cars; however, only about one-quarter said they regularly used marijuana in bars or other public places, and more than one-third said they never smoked in public places. Finally, the group was evenly divided on the issue of smoking in their parents' homes, with about half indicating that they smoked there at least occasionally and the other half saying they never did.

Even though marijuana played an important role in the social life of most of the subjects, with three-quarters describing most or all of their friends as also being regular users, a very high proportion (89%) said they regularly smoked while alone, and almost half of the total group (45%) said that most of the time they smoked they were alone. Spouses or partners also were frequently identified by subjects (76%) as people with whom they regularly smoked.

Table 15 presents an overview of the percentage of the total group using marijuana on a regular basis during various times of working and non-working days. As can be seen from these figures, for the majority of subjects marijuana use occurred throughout the days in which they did not work, with a smaller proportion smoking prior to dinnertime on working days.

From a 12-item list of reasons people sometimes use marijuana, the subjects most frequently identified seven reasons underlying their use of the drug:

Table 15. Percentage of Subjects Regularly Using Marijuana at Various Times of Working and Non-Working Days

Time of day	Working days	Non-Working days
At the start of the day	39.9%	69.8%
During the day	48.7%	90.5%
At dinnertime	89.4%	84.6%
In the evening	98.0%	98.7%
At bedtime	71.3%	77.7%

to get pleasure, to feel good, get high (99%)

to relax, relieve tension (97%)

to use with friends, to enjoy effects (88%)

to overcome depression (61%)

to enhance sexual interest or pleasure (60%)

for fun, kicks, excitement (57%)

to forget troubles (53%)

Slightly fewer than half of the subjects responded affirmatively to two additional reasons for using marijuana:

to deepen self-understanding (49%)

to produce intense exciting experiences (42%)

A quarter or less of the total group listed the remaining three items as reasons why they smoked marijuana:

to go along with what my friends are doing (25%)

to make me more satisfied with myself (21%)

to go along with what my partner or spouse is doing (20%)

As can be seen from the data in Tables 16 and 17, the subjects as a group were highly positive in their assessment of both the short-term and long-term effects of marijuana on their own lives and functioning. In contrast to nine aspects of functioning

Table 16. Short-Term Effects of Marijuana

Things one-half or more of the subjects said were made better	*Made worse*
Ability to relax and enjoy life (76.2%)	None
Enjoyment of food (72.8)	
Ability to sleep well (62.3)	
Ability to avoid boredom (60.9)	
Enjoyment of sex (59.6)	
Ability to avoid feeling angry (57.3)	
Enjoyment of recreational activities (57.0)	
Physical discomforts (53.6)	
Ability to avoid feeling depressed (50.3)	
Things one-third to one-half of the subjects said were made better	*Made worse*
Ability to have a good time with friends (47.0)	Memory (45.0)
Excitement and enthusiasm for life (47.0)	Ability to concentrate on complex tasks (40.7)
Ability to avoid feeling frustrated (45.6)	
Ability to be tolerant and considerate of others (43.3)	Ability to stay awake (35.8)
Ability to forget problems and troubles (43.0)	Ability to get things done (33.1)
Ability to understand yourself (39.1)	
Creativity (36.4)	
Relations with spouse or sex partner (35.8)	
Ability to understand other people (34.4)	
Things one-fifth to one-third of the subjects said were made better	*Made worse*
General satisfaction with life (30.4)	General level of energy (28.5)
General satisfaction with yourself (28.5)	
Relations with close friends (28.0)	Carefulness in driving and in potentially dangerous activities (24.7)
Self-control and ability to stay out of trouble (27.8)	
Ability to avoid shyness and feel at ease with other people (27.2)	Work performance (23.3)
Relations with co-workers and other acquaintances (27.2)	Ability to think clearly (32.2)
Relations with family members (other than parents) (21.2)	

Table 17. Long-Term Effects of Marijuana

*Things one-half or more of the subjects said
    were improved*
    Ability to overcome anxiety and worry (72.0%)
    Understanding of others (58.0)
    Creativity (57.7)
    Ability to enjoy varied and numerous
        activities (54.7)
    Self-understanding (54.0)
    Ability to enjoy life (53.6)
    Overall happiness (51.7)
    Ability to be tolerant and considerate
        of others (50.0)

Impaired
    Memory (66.7%)

*Things one-third to one-half of the subjects said
    were improved*
    General satisfaction with life (48.0)
    Relations with spouse or sex partner(s) (46.3)
    Excitement and enthusiasm for life (40.4)
    Ability to cope and solve life problems (40.3)
    Ability to avoid shyness and feel at
        ease with other people (39.9)
    Relations with co-workers and other
        acquaintances (39.1)
    Emotional stability (39.1)
    Relations with close friends (37.1)

Impaired
    Ability to con-
        centrate on
        complex tasks
        (48.7)
    Ability to get
        things done
        (47.7)
    Ability to think
        clearly (43.3)
    General level of
        energy ((42.7)
    Physical health
        (39.1)
    Ambition (36.0)

*Things one-fifth to one-third of the subjects said
    were improved*
    General satisfaction with yourself (31.3)
    Sense of purpose and meaning in your life (30.5)
    Ability to stick with tough situations
        and see them through (29.1)
    General self-confidence (27.8)
    Ability to work for and get things you want (26.5)

Impaired
    Educational prog-
        ress and
        achievement
        (31.3)
    Ability to get
        ahead in
        career (27.8)

Table 17.   Continued.

Self-control and ability to stay out of trouble (25.8) Work performance (20.0)	Ability to avoid accidents (25.2) Relations with parents (22.8)

that one-half or more of the group felt were usually made better on a short-term basis by marijuana, virtually nothing was identified by such a proportion of subjects as usually made worse. They were only slightly more negative in assessing marijuana's long-term effects, with more than two-thirds of the group identifying memory as being impaired.

Consistent with their evaluation of marijuana's positive effects, relatively few subjects indicated having had frequent negative reactions to smoking marijuana during the year preceding the time of their interviews. Only slightly more than 10 percent, for example, said they had frequently been worried while smoking marijuana because they did not know how people were reacting to them, and approximately 5 percent said that while smoking they frequently saw themselves as they really were and did not like what they saw. No other frequently occurring negative reaction was identified by more than 4 percent of the total group.

PSYCHOSOCIAL PROFILE

The responses the subjects provided to questionnaire items concerning their social behavior overall portrayed them as a fairly normative group. Although 60 percent said they had broken the law at some time in their lives, in almost every case, this referred to the possession, use, or sale of drugs. Only 8 percent had ever been arrested.

In responding to questions about their current patterns of social interaction, the large majority of subjects described themselves as having fairly active and pleasurable social lives. On the average they indicated going out between two and three nights per week for recreation and going out with a date or with their spouse or living partner an average of about once a week. More than 80 percent said that they got together informally with friends at least once a week, and as a group the subjects went to parties or other social affairs an average of approximately twice a month.

Almost two-thirds (62%) responded that they spent at least an hour of leisure time alone each day. A similar proportion described themselves as daily television viewers, with the average time spent watching television exceeding three hours per day for the entire group. Finally, approximately 60 percent of the group said that they worked around the house or yard for relaxation at least once a week, and almost half said they exercised by themselves on at least a weekly basis.

More than three-quarters of the entire group disagreed or mostly disagreed with the statement "I find I don't know what to do with a lot of my leisure time," and almost as many (71%) agreed or mostly agreed that "time seems to pass very quickly during my leisure hours." Fewer than 40 percent agreed or mostly agreed with the statement, "I feel that I waste a lot of my free time because I don't end up doing things that are either productive or enjoyable."

When asked to assess a number of specific things that may have influenced their happiness and satisfaction during the immediately preceding several weeks, the subjects overall indicated that things had been going quite well. In rating how they felt about 46 separate items, using a scale ranging from 1 ("terrible") to 7 ("delighted"), they averaged scores of 5.0 ("mostly satisfied") or better on 22 of the items (see Table 18). Another 22 items received average ratings of between 4.0 ("mixed") and 5.0 ("mostly satisfied"); only two items were rated as less than 4.0 (indicating dissatisfaction), and those were matters of personal income and the standards and values in today's society.

On a more general level, the subjects were asked to consider their feelings about their life overall and to rate on a scale of 1 ("Absolute bottom, could not be worse") to 10 ("Absolute top, could not be better,") how things were 1 year before the in-

**Table 18. Average Ratings of 46 Selected Aspects of
Happiness and Satisfaction**

Items receiving average ratings of 5.0 ("mostly satisfied") or better
1. Your liking for the actual work that is involved in your job (5.1)
2. The physical surroundings and working conditions in your job (5.1)
3. The amount of job security you have (5.0)
4. Your overall health (5.2)
5. Your religious life (6.4)
6. The enjoyment you experience when you are around other people (5.2)
7. Your ability to gain cooperation from other persons (5.3)
8. Your general enjoyment of life (5.0)
9. Your sensitivity to other persons' feelings (5.5)
10. The degree of love and acceptance you feel from others (5.1)
11. How you have handled problems that have come up (5.0)
12. Your ability to take it when things get tough (5.2)
13. The respect you get from others (5.3)
14. Your ability to adjust to changes that come along (5.4)
15. Your ability to get along with other people (5.7)
16. The amount of friendship and love in your life (5.1)
17. Your own family life (5.0)
18. The things you do and the times you have with friends (5.2)
19. Your ability to get things done efficiently (5.2)
20. Your ability to express your ideas to others (5.4)
21. Your ability to share your feelings with persons who are close to you (5.2)
22. Your ability to think things through and come up with good answers (5.6)

Items receiving average ratings of 4.0 ("mixed") to 5.0 ("mostly satisified")
1. Your overall satisfaction with your work (4.7)
2. The amount of pay you get for the amount of work you do (4.1)
3. Your overall physical condition (4.8)
4. The amount of time you have for doing things you want to do (4.5)
5. The chances you have for recreation and just taking it easy (4.7)
6. What you are accomplishing with your life (4.3)
7. Your ability to change things around you that you don't like (4.3)

Table 18.   Continued.

---

  8. Your ability to satisfy and meet your needs (4.5)

  9. How interesting your day-to-day life is (4.5)

10. The fullness and completeness of your love/sex life (4.4)

11. Your ability to handle your emotions and feelings (4.9)

12. How honest and sincere other people are with you (4.9)

13. Your standard of living (4.2)

14. How consistent and understandable your world seems to be (4.3)

15. How happy you are (4.7)

16. Your independence and freedom (4.9)

17. How much fun you are having (4.8)

18. The amount of intimacy and warmth in your life (4.7)

19. Your close relatives, parents, brothers, sisters, etc. (4.9)

20. Your prospects for a good life in the future (4.9)

21. Your success in getting ahead in the world (4.8)

22. Your ability to concentrate (4.2)

Items receiving average ratings of 3.0 ("mostly dissatisfied") to 4.0 ("mixed")

  1. The amount of income you have (3.4)

  2. The standards and values in today's society (3.2)

---

terview, how they were at present, and how they thought their life situation would most likely be 1 year later. The average rating of the group for how things were the previous year was 5.6, falling between "Good and bad aspects about even" (5.0) and "Somewhat good, good aspects slightly outweigh the bad" (6.0). At the time of the interviews the subjects rated their lives in general an average of 6.5, approaching a level of "Pretty good," (7.0) and slightly exceeding the average rating of 6.3, which, in response to a later question, they gave to the current lives of people they knew of the same age and sex. Projecting into the future, the group as a whole rated their lives in the subsequent year an average of 7.7, or close to "Actually quite good" (8.0). More than eight of every ten subjects (83%) saw an overall upward movement in considering the status of their lives over the three-year span.

    Responses to items in other sections of the questionnaire

provided a picture that confirmed these assessments in some respects and suggested important differences in others. Responding to a series of questions regarding their current jobs, for example, fewer than half of the group (42%) described themselves as "completely satisfied" or "quite satisfied" with their positions, and about one-quarter indicated they were dissatisfied. In addition, approximately 40 percent said they felt that they were advancing in their jobs or careers less quickly than were others of their age and sex, and only 23 percent felt they were advancing more quickly.

Answers to specific questions concerning their close relationships likewise revealed some previously unexpressed dissatisfactions. Among the two-thirds of the group who were involved in steady relationships with a partner at the time of the interviews, only about half described themselves as being highly satisfied. Similarly, among those who were parents, only 41 percent indicated feeling highly satisfied with their experience of being a parent, and 38 percent said they were dissatisfied. In even greater numbers, subjects who were not in a steady relationship at the time of their interviews evidenced considerable dissatisfaction with the "single life," with only one-quarter of this subgroup describing themselves as highly satisfied.

The subjects' relationships with their parents were an area of additional dissatisfaction, judging from their responses to open-ended questions on this topic. Only approximately one-quarter of the respondents characterized their relationship with their mothers as quite close, providing such descriptions as the following:

"Very open, honest loving relationship."
"We are very close, she's the dearest person in this world to me."
"She encourages me in every way."
"I admire her a great deal; good understanding and trust."
"Very supportive; our relationship is good."

A second subgroup of 37 percent of the subjects saw their relationships with their mothers as workable but with some problems. Typical of the descriptions provided by this group were such remarks as:

> "We used to fight terribly . . . steadily getting better."
> "Relationship is antagonistic, but I love her very much."
> "We had been extremely close, but she now lives in another world."
> "We get along when I'm not living at home."
> "We're close but can't really discuss things."

In the third subcategory 29 percent of the subjects characterized their relationships with their mothers as having marked difficulties, providing such descriptions as the following:

> "Phoney relationship. I don't really know her. She's a very neurotic person."
> "Typical woman—neurotic."
> "She's OK but crazy and I avoid her."
> "We speak occasionally, but nothing gets said."
> "She's paranoid and accusing—hard to get along with."

The remaining 9 percent of the subjects' mothers were deceased or altogether absent from the subjects' lives.

Relationships with fathers emerged as an area of even greater dissatisfaction among the subject group, with only 15% describing themselves as quite close to their fathers. Typical remarks provided by this group including the following:

> "He does as much as possible for his family. He's always made things good for me."
> "We're very close. I discuss all my personal problems with him."
> "Our relationship is open and honest."
> "He's understanding and has always given me the initiative to do what I wanted. I'm deeply indebted to him."

An additional 20 percent of the subjects characterized their relationships with their fathers as not generally close but workable, describing them in terms such as the following:

> "We get along well because we don't see each other too often."
>
> "We've had our differences, but I know his concerns are based on love."
>
> "We get along well but find it hard to be open and honest with each other."
>
> "We have a friendly relationship now. There was a lot of fear, resentment, and nothing in common earlier."
>
> "We've never had much communication but we love each other."

The largest proportion of the subjects, 40 percent, characterized their relationships with their fathers as generally problematic. Typical of the descriptions provided by this subgroup were the following:

> "He's prejudiced against everything I'm interested in."
>
> "He's alcoholic and we have a very slight relationship."
>
> "We speak only about three times a year."
>
> "We're not very close because of value differences."
>
> "Casual relationship—I rarely confide in him."

The remaining subjects, 25 percent, indicated that their fathers were deceased or that they had not had a relationship with them.

The exploration of the subjects' current psychological problems in several different sections of the questionnaire revealed some additional areas of difficulties, although here too responses were not entirely consistent. In one section the respondents were asked to rate a list of 20 problems and complaints that people sometimes have according to the degree to which they were currently bothered by that particular problem. As

**Table 19.   Average Ratings of 20 Selected
Psychological Problems**

---

*Items receiving average ratings of 1.0 ("bothered by this
problem not at all") to 2.0 ("bothered a little bit")*

 1. Nervousness or shakiness inside (1.9)
 2. The idea that someone else can control your thoughts (1.2)
 3. Feeling others are to blame for most of your troubles (1.5)
 4. Thoughts of ending your life (1.3)
 5. Hearing voices that other people do not hear (1.0)
 6. Suddenly scared for no reason (1.2)
 7. Temper outbursts that you could not control (1.4)
 8. Feeling that people are unfriendly or dislike you (1.5)
 9. Having to check and double-check what you do (1.8)
10. Difficulty making decisions (1.7)
11. Feeling hopeless about the future (1.7)
12. Feeling uneasy when people are watching or talking about you (1.8)
13. Having urges to beat, injure, or harm someone (1.4)
14. Having urges to break or smash things (1.5)
15. Feeling very self-conscious with others (1.8)
16. Spells of terror or panic (1.2)
17. Feelings of worthlessness (1.6)

*Items receiving average ratings of 2.0 ("bothered by this
problem a little bit") to 3.0 ("bothered moderately")*

 1. Feeling tense or keyed up (2.3)
 2. Feeling blue (2.4)
 3. Feeling most people will take advantage of you if you let them (2.1)

---

shown in Table 19, using a 5-point scale the subjects averaged scores of between 1 ("not at all") and 2 ("a little bit") on 17 of the 20 items. Only three problems—"feeling blue," "feeling tense or keyed up," and "feeling most people will take advantage of you if you let them"—received average ratings of slightly more than 2.0.

As a group, the subjects evidenced a fairly high degree of self-esteem in responding to several items that measured this variable and that were included in the same close-ended section of the questionnaire. Almost three-quarters, for example, re-jected the statement, "At times I think I am no good at all." More than two-thirds disagreed with the statement "I certainly feel useless at times," and only slightly fewer (56%) disagreed with "I wish I could have more respect for myself."

Elsewhere on the questionnaire, however, a somewhat different picture emerged, with 67 percent of the subjects respond-ing affirmatively to a question about whether they had experi-enced any persistent emotional or psychological problems and more than half (56%) indicating that at some point in their lives they had felt they were going to have or were close to having a "nervous breakdown." Almost two-thirds said someone had sug-gested to them that they see a psychiatrist, a psychologist, or a counselor, and 41 percent had actually seen someone.

The subjects' responses to an open-ended item later in the questionnaire, which asked them to describe the nature and du-ration of any present psychological problems, provided addi-tional information about this area. Here, six of every ten subjects indicated that they had been troubled over periods ranging from several months to many years by at least one such problem. The most frequently mentioned problem area concerned their feelings about themselves, with 15 percent describing them-selves as insecure, having a low self-image, overly introverted, and in a very few cases, feeling self-destructive or having a sense of self-hate.

Depression was the next most frequently mentioned prob-lem, with 14 percent identifying this as their primary trouble. Other areas included problems with relationships (serious dis-satisfaction with current relationship, fears of intimacy and commitment, lack of meaningful relationships in one's life, etc.), which were indicated by 9 percent; anxiety, mentioned by 5 per-cent; and problems with parents, identified by 3 percent. The primary problems indicated by the remaining 14 percent of the sample covered a wide range, including feeling violent, para-noid, angry, or out of control; having mood swings or "midlife crises" and experiencing difficulties making decisions.

When asked what they felt was the cause of the difficulties they were experiencing, only approximately one-third of those who had identified a significant problem area focused on them-

Table 20. Reasons Indicated for Use of Marijuana

Reasons for use of marijuana	All subjects (N = 150)	Selected subjects (N = 15)
To get pleasure, to feel good, get high	149 (99%)	15 (100%)
To relax, relieve tension	145 (97%)	15 (100%)
To use with friends, to enjoy effects	132 (88%)	14 (93%)
To overcome depression	92 (61%)	10 (67%)
To enhance sexual interest or pleasure	90 (60%)	9 (60%)
For fun, kicks, excitement	85 (57%)	7 (47%)
To get away from problems and troubles	79 (53%)	10 (67%)
To deepen self-understanding	74 (49%)	7 (47%)
To produce intense exciting experiences	63 (42%)	6 (40%)
To go along with what my friends are doing	37 (25%)	6 (40%)
To make me more satisfied with myself	31 (21%)	0 (0%)
To go along with what my partner or spouse is doing	30 (20%)	6 (40%)

selves as the source. Slightly more than half attributed their problems to a variety of external conditions or circumstances, including their childhoods or family relationships, their jobs or financial states, where or with whom they were currently living, or recent experiences such as an abortion or car accident. Somewhat fewer than 5 percent saw drugs as the primary cause of their psychological problems, and the remaining almost 8 percent pointed to such things as "fate" or "life forces" or said they did not know what had caused their problems.

From the large amount of information obtained from the questionnaires completed by the 150 subjects, a spectrum of daily marijuana-smoking adults emerged from which 15 individuals were selected to be studied more intensely, using a combination of interviews and psychological tests. As indicated in the previous chapter, the selected subjects were representative of the various types of heavy marijuana users seen among the larger group. Among the men who were chosen were a successful corporate attorney, a salesman, a photographer, a musician and part-time music teacher, a young accountant, a business manager for a newspaper, a freelance screenwriter, and a full-

**Table 21. Aspects of Life Experience Most Frequently
Described as Positively Affected by Marijuana[a]**

Aspects positively affected by marijuana	All subjects (N = 150)	Selected subjects (N = 15)
Ability to relax and enjoy life	114 (76%)	13 (87%)
Enjoyment of food	109 (73%)	11 (73%)
Ability to overcome worry and anxiety	108 (72%)	15 (100%)
Ability to sleep well	93 (62%)	10 (67%)
Ability to avoid feeling bored	91 (61%)	10 (67%)
Enjoyment of sex	90 (60%)	10 (67%)
Understanding of others	87 (58%)	12 (80%)
Creativity	87 (58%)	12 (80%)
Ability to avoid feeling angry	87 (58%)	9 (60%)
Ability to enjoy varied activities	82 (55%)	10 (67%)
Self-understanding	81 (54%)	11 (73%)
Overall happiness	78 (52%)	9 (60%)
Ability to avoid feeling depressed	75 (50%)	11 (73%)
Ability to be tolerant and considerate of others	75 (50%)	7 (47%)

[a]For the purposes of comparison, subjects' responses regarding short-term and long-term effects of marijuana have here been combined.

time graduate student. The seven women included a well-published writer, a suburban housewife and part-time manager of a small retail store, an administrative assistant in a large corporation, a secretary, a personnel manager, a medical technician, and a film maker.

In terms of age, educational level, religion, marital status, occupation and income, the subjects selected for intensive study closely matched the distributions of these variables among the full group of 150. In addition, they closely approximated the larger group in terms of the reasons they gave for their heavy, long-term use of marijuana. As shown in Table 20, the percentages of selected subjects indicating each of twelve reasons for using the drug was similar to those seen among all subjects. As seen in Table 21, the selected subjects also closely mirrored the total group in their assessments of the effects of marijuana on various aspects of life experience.

In the following chapter, six of the men and women we studied intensively are presented in detail. Here, special emphasis is placed on identifying both consistencies and differences between the information that the subject provided on the questionnaire and what was subsequently learned through the interviewing process and the psychological test findings.

CHAPTER 4

SELECTED CASES OF ADULT DAILY MARIJUANA USERS

Presented in this chapter are summaries of 6 of the 15 daily marijuana-smoking adults selected for intensive study from among the larger number of subjects who have been described in Chapter 3. These particular individuals are presented because they illustrate well the range of contexts in which we found daily marijuana use by adults to occur. In reading the cases it should be kept in mind that our focus in this study was on a type of marijuana smoker who had not previously been examined. Like all our subjects, these men and women had been daily users of marijuana for a considerable period of time, they were not patients, were not referred because of difficulties with the law, and at least on initial questioning saw marijuana as enhancing their lives.

The six cases run the gamut of demographic and socioeconomic variables seen in our larger group of 150. If all were united by marijuana smoking, what distinguished them was less social, economic, religious, or ethnic differences than distinctions based on the role marijuana played in their adaptation to work, in their primary relationships, and the way they related to their own situations and life circumstances.

DANIEL POLLOCK*

Screening Session and Questionnaire

Daniel Pollock was a short, well-built atorney of forty-four whose dress reflected the considerable financial success he had realized as a partner in a prestigious firm. A graduate of Harvard University and Harvard Law School, he had spent his entire life before school and since living in New York City. He had been married and divorced twice and had two children from his first marriage who lived with their mother and whom Dan saw on a fairly limited basis. For the past year and a half he had been living with a successful female business executive in her early thirties and characterized himself as being "completely satisifed" in this relationship.

He indicated in his responses to the questionnaire that he had not become a regular smoker until his mid-twenties, shortly after his first marriage. For the past 18 years he had smoked two to three marijuana cigarettes a day; however, on the questionnaire he indicated he was concerned about the effects of marijuana on his health and that he would like to cut down the amount he smoked. On working days he limited his use of marijuana to the after-work and evening hours and smoked throughout the day on weekends.

He claimed never to have had any bad reactions while high on marijuana and listed as key reasons for his use the effects it had on his ability to relax and enjoy life and to forget his troubles, his enjoyment of food and sex, his ability to be tolerant and considerate of others, and the fact that it improved his relationships with those around him.

Other than noting that he had frequent disagreements with his mother and describing himself as occasionally feeling "a little bit" tense or keyed up, he indicated on the questionnaire no problems or complaints in his current life. On a questionnaire scale of 1 to 10 he rated his life last year, this year, and next year as a 9 ("Very good, could hardly be better").

---

*All names and some of the identifying details in this chapter have been changed to protect the subjects.

Interviews

Although Dan was affable and talkative throughout each of his interviews, his speech and manner suggested a need to impress and to be admired. He saw himself as someone who had a great deal to contribute to our study and said at the outset that he put everything of himself into everything he did. Explaining that he was an "organized and fairly compulsive person," he said he wished to present his life in a logical fashion.

He related his use of marijuana to his being a driving, controlling, orderly person, saying that marijuana made him mellow and diminished his sense of competition. In his first interview he described himself as a benevolent despot at work, joking that he treated all his subbordinates equally—"like dogs." Another time he described himself as "legally ethical but a bastard" and said he would "go after someone for the last penny for the sake of my clients."

He made a point of saying, "I never work at home. I never make business calls; I make it a policy never to let my clients, except in extreme emergencies, call me at home. I have no friends who are lawyers. I divorce myself from law when I go home. I think I have two divergent personalities, two divergent lives. I never smoke grass during the day at the office or at any time I'm working. I never have, and I've smoked two to three joints a day for close to 20 years."

His desire for success was also expressed, he said, in sports. He still played competitive team sports, and although he had never been a great athlete, he now considered himself to be a better athlete than most of his friends because he had kept in shape. He frequently used sports images and allusions in describing various aspects of himself and his life.

Dan described in detail his first serious relationship with a woman and his two marriages. Striking in his description was the way he catalogued the defects in each of the women with no sense that he might have in any way contributed to the failure of these relationships. With both wives and with his earlier girlfriend he saw himself as having given more to the relationship than they had.

He viewed his first wife as having been a giving, caring

person prior to the birth of their two children. He described her as overwhelmed by being a mother, however, and complained that most of the child care had been left to him. During the latter years of their marriage, he said, all she did was eat and sleep, ending up 70 pounds overweight. He described his second wife, with whom he had been involved before leaving his first wife, as an efficient manager who was able to handle both a job and her children from a previous marriage but who was disparaging toward him and unable to be loving and involved. Both women smoked marijuana with him although not as much as he did. He said with some pride that despite his disappointment with them sex with both remained excellent until the end, and he credited marijuana with having made things more bearable in the last stages of both relationships.

One of the reasons he had always been drawn to marijuana was that it served as an aphrodisiac for him. He said he did not need it to stimulate his desire, but it enhanced his pleasure and made it last longer. Marijuana stimulated sexual fantasies of being with two women or having one woman watch him while he had sex with another. In the last years of both marriages he had had involvements with other women and had sometimes acted out these fantasies. More often he would talk about them with the woman he was with while they were having sex. Since becoming involved in his current relationship he felt that his erotic fantasies of other women had decreased.

He saw in this woman, Susan, a combination of the best qualities of each of his two former wives: she was loving and caring like his first wife and efficient and able to deal with life in the way his second wife had been. He said she was the first person who ever responded to his being caring, loving, and protective. He felt he was helpful to her and tried not to be overbearing by expressing his opinions on everything the way he often did with other people. He thought they might get married but felt strongly that children would spoil their relationship and did not want any. He believed that Susan's desire for children was not very strong and described her work as first in her life, coming even before her relationship with him.

Dan's children, a daughter fourteen and a son eleven, were a source of some frustration and disappointment to him. He felt that neither had ever approached their interests with any intensity or had the desire to be the best at what he or she did, nor had they done well in school. He said he got along with them when he was being entertaining, but if he tried to be serious they treated it as a lecture and stopped listening. "I don't consider myself a good—a great father, particularly to younger-age children," he noted. "My long suits are not patience, tolerance, and understanding of mistakes." He was aware that he was often too critical, controlling, and hard-driving with his children and felt he had to work hard to control himself when he was with them.

He related many of his attributes to his own upbringing. He was the only child in a Jewish family that was, in his words, "goal-oriented." His father had been a successful district attorney, state assemblyman, and state senator. While Dan was growing up, his father had suffered several heart attacks and had stopped working, although he was active in his synagogue and continued to help other people informally.

Dan's most vivid childhood memory was of being called to his father's bedside in the middle of the night when he was six. His father had suffered a severe heart attack, and his mother thought he would not survive. Although he did survive, Dan never forgot what his father told him that night: "You're a very good boy, but I want you to always remember one thing. Never stop running until you've crossed the goal line." He felt he had taken the lesson with him and had always approached life that way, giving himself fully to what he did and working to be the best at it. In talking about this, he paraphrased a line from Robert Browning: "Let your reach exceed your grasp, or what's a heaven for?"

He described his mother as a more cautious person than his father and as having been concerned he would be hurt. At the same time, he said, he had learned from her to be happy and cheerful. He recalled her having told him, "There are two ways to be—happy and sad. If you're sad, one, you're not fun around anyone else, and two, what are you doing for yourself?" He said he knew it sounded simplistic, but that was the philosophy he had always followed. If he did get a little down once in a while, he prided himself on having the resilience to snap back.

Dan stressed that his parents had never given him the feeling of being loved for his own sake. They constantly expected him to perform, to keep his room clean, to be polite, to be the very best at anything he did, and they were never fully satisfied with his achievements. If he got a 93 on a test and two other classmates got higher grades, their focus would be on the two who did better. When he was accepted at Harvard, Yale, and Princeton and received scholarship offers from two of the three schools, they wanted to know why he did not also get a scholarship to the third. His father was a perfectionist who would get angry if he ever disobeyed and would occasionally slap him hard across the face. In recalling this, Dan made a point of saying he had never struck either of his own children.

He said he had never seen any affection or demonstration of warmth between his parents, but neither had he ever heard them quarrel. Although he did not consider them to have been unhappy in their relationship, he saw them as having done their duty toward each other and toward him without much real involvement.

His father died when Dan was twenty, but his mother was still alive, and he would call her every day to avoid her reproaches if he failed to do so. She would call him at the office, and if she did not reach him would leave messages with his receptionist about how warmly he should dress or asking if he had worn his overshoes. When she spoke with him, he said, she would ask him questions in a "machine gun-like barrage" and constantly tried to tell him what to do "about the children, about Susan, about everything."

He once sent her a humorous Mother's Day card about Jewish mothers making their sons feel guilty. When he came to take her out to dinner she said that, of course, she had tried to make him feel guilty and that otherwise he would not be taking her out for Mother's Day.

Later that day at the Harvard Club she told the waiter that Dan had gone to Harvard. Moments later she commented to Susan that although Dan was good-looking he looked like a gargoyle compared to her husband. At another point in the evening Susan gently said something to him about his talking too loud, which he admitted he had been doing. Although his mother did not comment at the time, she called him the next day to let him know it was not right that Susan had pointed that out and claimed that she would never have criticized his father in such a way.

Dan felt that marijuana enhanced his perceptiveness about people and situations. He said that while high, "I feel that I come out with pearls of wisdom that are absolutely original, and I've had reenforcement from people who say, 'Hey, that's very perceptive.' I see things vividly. I can understand like a philosopher-king type. I guess that's what I would like to be, a philosopher-king. In the office I rule with an iron hand. With grass, I become a pussy cat."

He indicated that he did not like to be alone, explaining, "I like people around. I guess I play off people better. I think I've always been an activist—an activity-oriented person. I never sit and just think for thirty minutes. If something's on my mind then I want to do something about it."

He went on to say, "I talk with my hands. When I'm in my office I walk up and down. It's not easy for me to sit still without moving or talking for long periods of time. I love talking, but I don't like to be immobile or passive. I prefer to have people around with whom to interact. I think that makes me feel more alive. I guess—in the extreme way I think—that if I'm all alone it's a sign that I could be dead."

In discussing his use of leisure time he noted, "Reading is not a relaxing or enjoyable activity, which is really an embarrassing thing to say with my educational background. I read at work, as you do, I'm sure. I don't get any pleasure, however, out of reading, whether it's legal or nonlegal material. In fact, until two years ago I had not read a book for over a dozen years."

In addition to not reading and not liking to be alone, he indicated that he never remembered his dreams and that despite his intensity he tried never to take things seriously. Together with the way in which he described his marriages, this appeared to indicate a desire both to stand back from people and events and to avoid looking at himself introspectively. His response to having this called to his attention was to comment on the interviewer's perceptiveness, a response that was in keeping with his need to keep distance.

When the interviewer pointed this out, he said, "I have two

choices—to believe what you said and cut my throat or to say, 'Screw you,' and forget it." When questioned about the strong imagery, he became quite animated and related it to his being a perfectionist. He felt that if he were a certain way at this time in his life, he was not going to change, and said facetiously, "What should I do—put a bullet in my head?" He hastened to add that the last thing he would ever do would be to kill himself. He went on to say that marijuana made it unnecessary for him to look at himself or to see any flaws.

When seen for two follow-up sessions 28 months later, Dan was tan and a little thinner. He talked first about having stopped smoking marijuana. He had found nine months ago that he was smoking it all day on weekends and more during the week than he ever had. He had been reading about its harmful effects, decided to try to stop, and had not smoked since. He claimed not to see any significant effect on his life but did state that he did not have sex as often. Although he and Susan used to have sex five times a week, it was now down to once or twice. He said the quality of their sexual relationship was still as good as it had always been and that he found it just as exciting, but that he was "not turned on as often." He was troubled by this diminution of desire and wondered whether perhaps he should go back to marijuana occasionally. He said that Susan had discouraged him from doing so.

Since marijuana's effect on his ability to relax had been an important part of his reason for smoking it, he was asked about the effects of his abstinence on this aspect of his life. He replied by stating that Susan's firm had moved to Connecticut, so she now came home an hour or two after he did. This gave him time alone to take a shower and get ready for the next day, and he felt that by having a chance to indulge his needs for cleanliness, neatness, and orderliness, he was able to unwind. He said it might also be that he was able to relax more because of Susan, or that perhaps he should give himself more credit. He said he was still the same irrascible, driving person in the office, and staying away from marijuana had not had an effect on his productivity at work. He added that he did not have the "munchies" as frequently as he had before and felt that had been responsible for his having lost a few pounds.

When he first stopped smoking, he said he would at times

take a drink to unwind but had stopped doing that. He also had used cocaine on an average of once every month or six weeks, whereas previously he had used it only a few times in his life. He described himself as using it in a compulsive way, finishing all he had as soon as he got it.

He talked of the changes in his relationship with Susan, describing it as having become closer and saying he was much happier about it. He said he was thinking about getting married in the next year and gave as one reason the problem unmarried people have with leases. He explained that he and Susan had talked about this, and he felt it was as good a reason as any to get married.

Dan said his relationship with his children also had improved, describing it as having been a 2 on a scale of 1 to 10 and moving up to a 6. His children had started in therapy, and he had gone to several sessions with each of them. He also had been to some joint sessions with his first wife and son. During one session the therapist asked him if he thought he could have lunch with his son without either making suggestions or asking him questions. He reported that they subsequently had had lunch together, and he felt very pleased that he had been able to do that. He said the boy also had seemed happy about it. He seemed aware that they got along much better when he was not continually evaluating things regarding his son in the ways his parents had always done with him. In spite of these improvements, he continued to see his children only every third weekend and to speak to them only occasionally on the phone. He said he was just too busy for any more contact but felt he was managing to be an effective parent, giving as an example the fact he was in the process of arranging to change his son's school.

When asked if there had been any change or improvement in his relationship with his mother, he quickly and humorously replied, "No, it's worse." Despite being busy, he said he still managed to call her every day. Not smoking had not led him to read any more than he had previously, nor had he started to recall his dreams since he stopped smoking.

Psychological Tests

Dan approached the psychological test session with the same forceful gregariousness he had consistently shown in his interviews, and he related to the examiner with what appeared to be a superficial style of friendliness. On the first test administered, the WAIS-R, his full scale IQ of 123 placed him within the superior range of functioning.

As shown in the following protocol, his scaled scores on the verbal part of the intelligence test ranged from a low of 12 on Information and on Similarities to a high of 18 on Vocabulary.

Verbal IQ = 130 (Very Superior)		*Performance IQ = 105 (Average)*	
Information	12	Picture Completion	12
Digit Span	14	Picture Arrangement	12
Vocabulary	18	Block Design	8
Arithmetic	15	Object Assembly	6
Comprehension	16	Digit Symbol	11
Similarities	12		

Dan's Vocabulary score of Very Superior suggested an exceptional ability to learn, understand, and accumulate verbal information, but as his other scores were somewhat lower, it was thought that some deterioration of functioning had taken place. On the Similarities subtest, which is considered particularly sensitive to impairment, he produced several answers that showed deficits in his reasoning process. To "eye-ear," for example, he responded, "parts of the face," and his response to "fly-tree" was "exist in picnic settings." His difficulties in the Information area related primarily to problems with numerical concepts. For example, he estimated the distance from New York to Paris to be 7,000 miles and the population of the United States to be 65 million. He also had minimal knowledge of scientific facts, identifying Madame Curie as having "developed the X-ray," and he was unable to name three types of human blood vessels.

In the Performance section of the WAIS-R his score of 105 was within the average range. The 25-point discrepancy between his Verbal and Performance IQ scores is statistically significant for individuals in Dan's age range ($p = .01$) and, as such, represents a real difference in cognitive functioning on the two sections of the WAIS-R (Naglieri, 1982).

Dan's best performances in the latter section were in Picture

Arrangement and Picture Completion, indicating knowledge of social relations and an ability to attend to fine details; his worst scores were in Object Assembly and Block Design. His difficulties here were due to problems in spatial organization and the construction of visual patterns. During this part of the testing he repeatedly pointed out that he was poor in these types of tasks. He frequently became frustrated by the difficulties he encountered but reassured himself by commenting that he felt he had functioned well in the verbal areas.

The MMPI report provided the following outline of Dan's personality: "This subject apparently has an intense need to appear in a good light. He lacks insight into his own behavior and denies unfavorable traits both to himself and to others. His tendency to misinterpret the intentions of others leads to interpersonal friction and handicaps him in social situations. His personality characteristics are stable and quite resistant to change."

When asked to draw a picture of a person, Dan provided a simple stick figure of a man (Figure 1) that, although minimal, conveyed action and reflected a high level of energy. This energy, however, was sometimes felt to move in the direction of agitated thoughts, judging from Dan's treatment of the figure's hair. The "tacked-up" smile on the drawn male's face was considered to imply a superficial agreeability and the need to play a likable role, and the closed eyes suggested the desire to avoid introspection or awareness of life's complications.

Dan described the male figure as follows: "It's a male, happy, going forward, and this is an attempt to mask my absolute inability to draw. No extra clothing, nothing. Exactly as I like to see myself. This person is ageless, between seven or eight and sixty. He's going to join others in a small group. He feels good with the pleasure and anticipation of being with others he likes. There's a certain carefree, unfettered, happy feeling. He joins his friends at the beach, and they relax and enjoy themselves. He's an attorney. He lives with someone with whom he's extremely happy, with a view toward eventual marriage, but not necessarily. He lives happily ever after." Dan commented that there was a 99 percent similarity between this description and himself.

His picture of a woman (Figure 2) also was a crude stick fig-

Figure 1.

ure with hastily drawn hair and two small circles along each side of the single-line body that Dan indicated were breasts. The dissociated, appendage-like quality of the breasts suggested that Dan perceived sex as something that was not well integrated into his relationships. The female figure's eyes were thought to reflect anger and, together with the eyebrows over them that erupted into jagged lines, sugested a measure of hostility not seen in his drawing of a male.

When asked to describe the woman he had drawn, however, Dan again related a simple, carefree tale: "The person has a good, happy attitude toward life. She is giving. Doesn't brood on the past. She's between seventeen or eighteen and sixty. I see her as a sexual object. But I'm not into young girls. The only distinguishing characteristic between man and woman are the breasts and hair. Right now she's walking, happy by herself but looking forward to meeting other people. She meets me as I'm walking

Figure 2.

along, and we join our friends at the beach. We go off and walk by ourselves." Dan concluded that the woman he drew was the one with whom he was currently living.

Dan provided a total of 20 responses to the Rorschach cards. The computer analysis (see Appendix for details) showed two aspects of his responses to be highly significant. First, his unusually high number of whole responses (10) in relation to only 2 responses in which human movement was perceived indicated an abnormally high level of aspiration and need to achieve. Second, his large number of responses (7) that used the achromatic portions of the blot as color (e.g., black, white, or gray) pointed to a significant level of anxiety, apprehension, and tension, and feelings of doubt and uncertainty.

The examiner rated 16 of Dan's 20 responses (80%) as having good form and the rest as adequate, showing him to be in good contact with reality. His low number of responses involving humans (2), however, was felt to be indicative of a lack of empathy and connection to others.

Content analysis of his responses further reflected an underlying disturbed self-image and in particular a sense of himself as overly burdened. Card 1, for example, was seen as "a moth trying to become a butterfly, with the head of a frog, possessing giant wings—wings too burdensome for the body, too bulky to be moving." The cartoon figure perceived in Card 5 was likewise described as "too bulky to be in motion," and Card 6 elicited "a goose flying. There's a feeling of mass. It's overwinged." Also evident were suggestions of self-damage, as in the perceptions of Card 10 of "a lobster with a claw cut off."

Sexual anxiety was suggested by his response to Card 2:"At the base the red part looks like a vagina—what a dominating woman's would look like, with stiletto-type things coming out, with rockets, threatening-looking." His perception of Card 10 as "the first Roscharch transvestite," with "a penis between the legs" and "wearing a bra," further suggested sexual conflict, expressed in a characteristically grandiose style.

Throughout Dan's Rorschach protocol, responses that reflected underlying disturbances were couched by playful perceptions and childlike references—clowning animals, cartoon characters, and happy children—suggestive of his need to deny unhappiness or difficulty. A comment made to the examiner following Card 9—"Have you noticed I don't see anything as being unhappy? That must be bad"—appeared to reflect his self-consciousness over the efforts he had made to appear light-hearted.

Summary

The questionnaire responses, the psychological test results, and the clinical picture that emerged through the unstructured interviews were strongly congruent in Dan's case. His denial of any real emotional or psychological difficulties on the questionnaire and his characterization of his life as one that "could hardly be better" suggested a determination to present himself as an unburdened, happy-go-lucky individual. Consistent with this, his simple stick figure drawings, with the repeated insistence on the happiness of the people in the stories he made up, set the tone for a testing profile of someone who was trying to see himself as content while not looking at himself too closely. At the same time, the testing revealed the presence of unadmitted self-doubt and a largely unconscious sense of being burdened, perhaps by the weight of having to maintain the facade he had constructed around himself.

On the Rorschach his low number of perceptions involving humans was seen as indicative of interference with his ability to empathize with others. His overriding need to achieve, tension, and conflicted sexuality—features emphasized in the Rorschach analysis—were all consistent with the clinical report.

His surprising lack of general information revealed by the WAIS-R, in someone with his education and high IQ, suggested a deterioration from a previous higher level of functioning. This is less startling in light of his statement in the interviews that he had virtually excluded all reading from his life for many years.

Dan appeared to have utilized well the advantages and opportunities of his life and to have repressed, denied, or compensated for the more painful aspects of his childhood. His obsessive, driven personality, which manifested in his unrelenting need for success, was part of the price he paid. In his pursuit of well-being and pleasure he cultivated the narcissistic aspects of his personality while attempting to overcome his driven, compulsively aggressive side. Marijuana seemed to help him in this attempted transformation, but his intellectual interests appeared to have been sacrificed in the process.

The interviews helped elaborate how marijuana also served as a stimulus to his sexual fantasies. The excitement he derived from being observed by another woman during sex or from fantasizing such observation reflected the narcissistic side of his character. The presence of two women also seemed to serve to limit his closeness to either. Since he had stopped smoking marijuana, he had felt a diminution in his sexual desire and appeared to want the interviewer's approval to resume, something he seemed likely to do in any case.

His inability to accept flaws in his children, other people, or himself led him to criticize others while avoiding introspection or self-criticism. His not reading books, which inevitably stimulates introspective comparison of one's life with the lives of those about which one reads, appeared to be related to this avoidance. Marijuana smoking seemed related to his need not to look closely at himself or his relations with other people.

He went through two marriages seeing only the faults of his wives and with no sense of any contribution he may have made to the failure of the relationships. Although he currently had a better relationship, the very closeness he was experiencing seemed to be motivating him to resume distancing himself with marijuana.

EMILY LEONE

Screening Session and Questionnaire

Emily Leone was a thirty-six-year-old woman who had recently married for the second time following a 13-year marriage in which she had had two girls, currently aged eleven and seven. Short, dark-haired, and attractive, she had been brought up in an Italian Catholic family in the Bronx. Since the time of her first marriage she had been living in a rural–suburban area of an upstate New York county and had a part-time job as the manager of a small retail store.

Emily first tried marijuana at the age of nineteen; within one year she had become a daily smoker and had remained so over the past 15 years. Although she did not usually smoke large quantities of marijuana, she began most days by getting high and smoked just enough throughout the day to maintain the effects. She sold marijuana to her friends and often smoked with them.

Her questionnaire responses revealed that she saw marijuana as making her more understanding and tolerant of others, enhancing her sexual interest and pleasure, helping her to relax and enjoy life, increasing her ability to cope with and solve life's problems, and helping her to avoid feeling angry, depressed, or bored. Except for indicating some unhappiness over the amount of her family's income (approximately $5,000 per year from her

job and $25,000 from her husband's job as a computer pro-
grammer), she characterized herself as "mostly satisfied" with all
aspects of her life, including her relationships with her husband
and children. Seeing the current year as an 8 on a questionnaire
scale of 1 to 10, she projected that next year would be a 10.

Interviews

Emily was lively, involved, and cooperative, and she spoke
relevantly about herself and her life. She began by giving a 5-
minute summary of her life, stating that she had been raised as a
Catholic, sent to parochial school, and brought up to do what
she was told. As a consequence, she said, at the age of nineteen
she married a man who was physically abusive to her but whom
she obeyed. After 13 years of marriage and the birth of her second child, she said she had experienced a transformation in her
life. She left her marriage, became her "own person," and now
described herself as very happy in a second marriage.

Prior to her first marriage she went out with her fiancé
three nights a week, but her parents required her to be home by
10 o'clock. He would spend the rest of the evening with his
friends, and she assumed that was where he learned to smoke
marijuana. He introduced her to the drug on their honeymoon
in the Caribbean. Neither of them had been on a plane before,
or in a hotel, or even in a formal dining room, and she said they
both needed marijuana to face the other people at dinner in the
hotel.

Early in her marriage she and her husband smoked socially
for the most part. By the end of the first year, however, both of
them were smoking every day. Emily saw marijuana as having
kept her mellow and less bothered by her husband's orders, in-
sults, criticisms, and physical abuse.

Marijuana was also an integral part of their sexual life together, and they never had sex except after smoking. She said
the sexual relationship was the best aspect of her first marriage
and described how she and her husband would get high, would
sometimes take Quaaludes or amphetamines, and "the sex
would go on all night." At times they dressed in costumes and
engaged in "limited bondage" in which they would tie each other

up. She felt her husband wanted to please her sexually, and she felt she had more control of their relationship when they were sexually involved than at any other time.

Emily said that she and her older daughter, Terry, had a special relationship that developed during the four years before her second daughter was born. Getting so little from her marriage, she put a great deal into her relationship with Terry. The child was intelligent, she said, and they could talk together and discuss their feelings about everything.

Her younger daughter, Lucy, who was now seven, was a more demanding and difficult child. Emily described the fights Lucy had had with her father as "contests of wills" in which he would end up throwing her onto the couch if she would not do what he wanted. Although Lucy had earlier been an angry child who had difficulty with her playmates, Emily said she had calmed down considerably since Emily's second husband had been part of her life.

She described her own parents as lacking in warmth. As she described her relationship with them, "It was important to them that I was obedient, did not get into trouble, was clean and orderly about my room, took care of my body, and that was it." She said neither she nor her younger sister were ever embraced. She could not talk to her parents about anything and said she had been hit frequently and "unconscionably hard" by her mother. One of her earliest memories was of being slapped across the face by her mother while they were in a grocery store.

Emily recalled that it was a tradition at Italian weddings for the father and the bride to dance together but that she and her father did not dance at her wedding because neither of them would have been comfortable being that close to each other. She did not see her parents as having been warm or affectionate with each other. They never quarreled, she said, "they just sort of existed."

Her father worked as a printer for most of his life. They had a hard time financially, and her mother worked part-time as a secretary for a funeral home. In recent years her father worked for the same firm taking care of the grounds. He liked the outdoor work, and it was the first time Emily could recall that he seemed satisfied with his work.

She and her sister, who was 23 months younger, were fiercely competitive and never close. Emily seemed to have had the better end of the competition because she was attractive, thin, had nice hair and did well in school, whereas her sister was plain, obese, had kinky hair, and did poorly in school. Emily said her sister was always being compared unfavorably to her by the family and by their teachers. Her sister had had an abortion as a teenager and subsequently had become addicted to heroin. She had recovered and gone on to marry a man who was disapproved of by her parents. She now had a child and lived near Emily, but although their children played together, she and her sister had remained distant.

She saw herself as never having been rebellious in any way. She had dated only one man since she was thirteen and had been expected to marry him. She said he had hit her even before they were married, but she had been ashamed to tell her parents about it.

Emily attributed breaking out of the marriage to wanting a better life for her two daughters. It was particularly intolerable to her that her husband beat her in front of the children. Her children went to a progressive suburban school where the students were made to feel important and not simply expected to obey. She talked to people at the school about her life and came to think of herself as a battered wife. Now she was herself involved in an organization that aided battered wives.

She described her husband as having been particularly difficult during the period when she was separating from him. At one point he put a gun to her head and threatened to shoot her if she moved. He was "insanely jealous" and told her she would never live to be with another man.

She had had a brief affair in the last months of her marraige, and although the relationship with this man did not last, she said it helped to give her the impetus to leave her husband. She felt the man's interest had cooled because of his fear of her ex-husband. She described herself as also having been intensely afraid her husband would find out about the affair, and some of this apprehension appeared to have remained and was reflected in the way she currently spoke about this episode.

Her husband disappeared during the period of their separation and had never been heard from since. Her younger daughter had been open about her pain and disappointment over the loss of her father, but her older daughter, who had actually been closer to him, had kept her feelings to herself.

She described her current husband, Greg, as sensitive and understanding and as her best friend in addition to being her lover. He had been married before and had two children who lived with his ex-wife. He got along with Emily's children, but they clearly regarded him as their stepfather and not as a replacement for their own father.

Emily's only complaint about Greg was that she wished he were more romantic. He did not say, "I love you," as often as she did. When they first met, she recalled, "We could not keep our hands off each other," and she regretted that their relationship was now less passionate. Although her first husband also had not been romantic, sex between them had continued to be exciting. She thought there might be more excitement in her sex life with Greg if they were both high on marijuana; but he did not smoke, and she said it would be of no use for her to be high if he were not. She wondered too if her first husband's continuing sexual passion was related to his having been psychologically disturbed in some way.

She said she put the children first in her life, above her husband, above everything else. She found being with them a strain, however, because of their bickering, quarreling, and demands. If she had her life to do over again, she said, she would not have had children and might not even have married.

Emily explained that smoking marijuana made her more relaxed and better able to deal with the children. On one occasion, however, when the interviewer called her to schedule a session and her older daughter answered the phone, the dialogue between them as the girl attempted to call Emily to the phone made it evident that she was high on marijuana and "spaced out" in talking to her child. When this was brought up in her next session, she revealed that her older daughter objected to her smoking and often urged her to stop.

Emily usually smoked marijuana in small amounts throughout the day to maintain its effect on her. In her first marriage she had needed marijuana to make the situation more tolerable, which raised the question of her need for it now. She felt marijuana heightened her awareness of things and mellowed her. It also made the ordinary situations in life, like housework, easier to cope with, she said.

Her present husband, Greg, accepted her smoking although he rarely smoked himself. She said that if she had the choice of smoking alone, with friends, around her children, or around Greg, her last choice would be smoking around her husband. She felt that somehow her smoking put them on "different wave lengths," which made her uncomfortable.

Emily wondered if marijuana interfered with her ambition. Although she worked in an organization for battered women, and lectured in a program at a local high school in addition to her job in the store, she thought that were she not smoking she might pursue her interests more vigorously and perhaps would get an education that would enable her to do more.

She and Greg had relatively little time alone. She was busy with her outside activities, the children, or housework. They spent a lot of time with friends, however. She described herself as feeling she had to "make up for lost time" from her earlier years and tended to overschedule herself. She speculated that maybe when she was a little older she might be able to just relax with her husband. She said that when they were alone most of their talking was about the things she did, and that he did not talk too much about himself or his work.

She and Greg had agreed that they should be free to have affairs with other people, which she referred to as cashing in their "fantasy tickets." They talked a good deal about this, and although she thought such affairs would not interfere with their marriage, she knew it was a risk but was prepared to take it in any case. In describing her views on sex outside marriage she said, "I feel about sexual adventures that if your life is running from here to there and it's, you know, just surviving and coping with all of the stuff that is going on in the world, if you step outside left or right of your life with someone, share a special hour or two and just escape totally, mentally, and physically from the norm, it's like recharging a battery, you know, and then you get back on the treadmill." She added that both she and Greg liked having their fantasy tickets be an active part of their relationship because otherwise they would feel they were giving up their independence.

She and Bill, the man with whom she had an affair toward the end of her first marriage, had joked about getting together again, and she believed that sooner or later they would. After her first interview she had a dream in which she was in the back of an open pickup truck with Bill. Greg was driving and a friend of Emily's was in the front seat with him. Emily and Bill were whispering even though her husband knew they were there.

Emily was attracted physically to Bill. He was tall and muscular, and when she kissed him she looked up to him; whereas her husband was her own height. Nevertheless, she said she had never had a better sexual relationship than she had with Greg.

When asked if she would feel more comfortable cashing in her fantasy tickets if she knew that her husband was doing so also, she agreed, adding that she would like him to do it first. He had a skin disease, however, that caused his skin to sag and made him look as if he had lost weight. She thought it would be hard for him to approach a woman and have an affair, whereas men did approach her.

Emily came to the third session in a low-cut, tight-fitting blouse and related a dream that she had had after the last interview. In the dream Greg called to tell her he loved her and was behaving in a manner she had indicated she wished he would in real life. In discussing the dream she returned to the theme of the passion that had been missing in their relationship and of her fantasy tickets.

She said that one of her fantasies was being "gently raped in a situation where you're not going to be killed or harmed." She described this imagined encounter as "something against your will but which turns out to be erotic and nice anyway."

One fantasy ticket that she said she had already cashed in involved participating in a threesome. Shortly after separating from her first husband she became sexually involved during the course of a weekend with a couple she was visiting. She had later discussed with Greg the possibility of the four of them having an involvement, and although he said he would be willing, she felt he might be uncomfortable seeing her with another man. She thought she would enjoy watching him with another woman.

She related another dream she had had the previous night

in which she and another woman were working with some black people who were "down and out" to help them make something of their lives. She felt attracted to one of the black men. In discussing the dream it emerged that a sexual experience with a black man was one of the fantasy tickets she would like to cash.

Speaking of blacks led her to think of the compassion she said she had had since she was little for those who were victims or helpless. She recalled that as a child she could not tolerate going fishing with her father, saying that what had troubled her the most was the "thought of hooking a worm and just having this thing be in pain before it drowns and then hooking a fish and seeing it just flopping around."

This brought her to the subject of death. Remarking that "I think of death all the time," she went on to explain that "I'm at this point where if I pass a spider web and see a fly getting caught, I'll take it out."

As the interviews progressed, she spoke of her preoccupation with death. She worried every day about her own death and always pictured is as violent: her first husband would come back and kill her or she would have an accident. She worried that she would die before her children were prepared to deal with life or that something would happen to them. She found it painful to think that her own death would not be noticed, saying, "Somehow all the lights in the country ought to go out for a minute or two to mark the occasion." She also wondered whether she would get a call that her mother, who was overweight and in bad health, had died. She said this thought was particularly upsetting to her because she felt that she and her mother had never really talked and she still hoped they would.

When seen one year after her initial series of interviews, Emily had recently quit her job at the store. She had worked there for 3 years and felt it was time to get a regular nine-to-five job with better pay. When she talked about actually having such a job, however, it was without pleasure or enthusiasm. She seemed to perceive it as a form of regimented responsibility, adding that it was a matter of growing up, and she thought it might be time that she did. For now she was finding it nice to have the summer off to relax and to go away occasionally with her children and her husband.

She thought she might have to take a regular job for only a

year because her first husband would soon have been missing for five years. This meant that he would be declared legally dead and that she would be entitled to the insurance. Because that promised to be a considerable sum of money, she anticipated that it would not be necessary for her to have to work.

She appeared to have abandoned any long-term career aspirations, saying that anything she would really want to do, such as working with adolescents, would require her to go to school and that this would be too much of a commitment and too much of a restriction on her freedom. As long as she did not really need the money, she felt she would rather work as a volunteer somewhere.

Following the sudden death of her mother's younger brother a few months earlier, Emily and her mother did have the talk that she wanted. He had had a heart attack while driving, the car crashed, and both he and his wife were killed. Emily drove her mother several times to visit the family and to make arrangements for the funeral, which gave them a chance to talk. Her mother complained that she had been the last to know that Emily was being abused by her first husband. She told her mother that she was ashamed to let her know but did not tell her how upset she had been about having been beaten by her when she was a child. Emily knew that her mother did not recognize that she had abused her and indeed believed that Emily should spank her children more.

She realized that her husband had cashed in a fantasy ticket while away on a trip, becoming sexually involved with a woman for one night. After he told her, they talked about it a lot for three days, but she said that it had not interfered with their relationship. She denied feeling any jealously and wondered if she and Greg had "something so special that we can do that kind of thing." She was asked whether, now that Greg had cashed a fantasy ticket, she was planning to do the same thing. She admitted that she was. She described having met a man in connection with her former work, with whom she had spoken about having a sexual involvement. She said she would see him this week and that there was a good chance that they would become involved.

By the next time she was seen, one week later, the involvement had occurred. They had met at a motel the previous night, and she had brought marijuana and a bottle of wine. The talked, drank, and smoked. She said he behaved "more like a woman," saying they probably would not have sex that night because he was tired, but they eventually did. The man was not particularly passionate, however, and Emily said the sex was more exciting in the anticipation than in reality—in choosing her clothes, shaving her legs, painting her nails, and getting ready in ways she no longer did with her husband. She intended to tell Greg and was confident he would not be upset. She planned to continue to see this man every month or so, unless it became clear that it would jeopardize her marriage.

She recalled feeling while driving to the motel that she would enjoy the evening more if she just went home and spent it with Greg, but she felt she had to prove something and went ahead. Asked what she had to prove, she replied, "That I was still free, that nothing could stop me, not even me."

She was still smoking as much marijuana as she had before and was continuing to sell it to friends. She said her younger daughter was now objecting to her smoking and occasionally flushed her marijuana cigarettes down the toilet. Her older daughter had dropped the subject, and Emily suspected that she might have taken up smoking herself. She wondered how she would feel about it if her suspicion turned out to be true, saying it would be a test of her values with regard to marijuana. At the same time, however, she felt Terry was too young to smoke. She said she had talked with the children directly about her smoking and that they knew that she made some extra money by selling marijuana. She had told them she would not embarrass them by smoking around their friends and said she also tried not to smoke around them. As a result, she was smoking more when she was alone, particularly when when she was driving or before the children came home from school.

Psychological Tests

Emily was pleasant, cooperative, and relaxed throughout the testing. On the WAIS-R she demonstrated superior intelligence, obtaining a Full Scale IQ of 127. Her verbal IQ was 122, and her performance IQ was 124, reflecting no significant differences in cognitive functioning as measured by the two areas on the test. On the 11 subtests of the WAIS-R, where a score of 10 is about average, she scored as follows:

Verbal IQ = 122 (Superior)		*Performance IQ = 124 (Superior)*	
Information	12	Picture Completion	12
Digit Span	16	Picture Arrangement	15
Vocabulary	12	Block Design	11
Arithmetic	11	Object Assembly	12
Comprehension	15	Digit Symbol	13
Similarities	13		

On the Verbal section, she did best in Digit Span and Comprehension. This indicated that she was able to attend to stimuli and that she had an excellent understanding of the world about her. On the other hand, her poorest performance was in Arith-

Figure 3.

Figure 4.

metic, showing difficulties in or lack of desire regarding concentration. In the Performance area, she did best in Picture Arrangement, suggesting excellent understanding of social situations. She did poorest in Block Design, which indicated difficulties in working with objects in space, such as would be involved in mechanical activities.

The MMPI report provided the following outline of Emily's personality: "This subject's approach to the MMPI was open and cooperative. The resulting profile is valid and probably a good indication of her present level of personality functioning. Although she appears to be very self-confident, she may overevaluate her capabilities and overextend herself with projects or activities that she has difficulty completing. She appears to be quite optimistic about her future and may outwardly deny problems and look on the brighter side even in the face of problems. Generally spontaneous and expressive, she may also be a bit impulsive, preferring action to reflection and tending to be somewhat indifferent to details. She seems to enjoy taking risks and has a low level of anxiety. She tends to be quite competitive, and may be rather aggressive and dominant in social relationships. She values autonomy and independence. Quite outgoing and sociable, she has a strong need to be around others. Although she is gregarious and effective at gaining recognition from others, her personal relationships may be somewhat superficial."

On the Draw-A-Person Test, Emily produced two figures (Figures 3 and 4) with an immature appearance. The arms on both figures extended to the side at almost right angles to the body, suggesting a mixture of openess and immobility. Psychosexual difficulties were indicated by the unmodulated, somewhat chaotic lines used to shade the man's shorts and the emphasis on the fly, the absence of identifiable sexual characteristics in the female, and the exaggeratedly long neck of the female, which suggested an attempt to distance her awareness (head area) from her bodily impulses. The male, in particular, was not well-balanced on the ground, and both figures had feet too small for the person drawn, a further sign of inadequate stability. The hair treatment reflected wildness around the head, suggesting mental agitation.

Emily's description of the female figure was as follows: "This is a woman in a good mood without shoes. She's wearing jeans and a T-shirt, no makeup, no jewelry. She's informal. She might be a mother with children and no spouse. She's smiling because her two kids are in school, finally. Her open arms are welcoming the day. She holds odd jobs, part-time jobs, nothing very regimented. For example, she might bake at home for restaurants, such as I've done. In the future she identifies who she is. As the kids need her less, she educates herself more. Her goal is to be helpful in the community. She holds down a good job and probably gets involved in social services."

This story appeared to be autobiographical, at least to a degree, reflecting Emily's view of herself having been divorced, having two children, and working at odd jobs. It also seemed to represent her desire for an informal approach to life, as conflict-free as possible, yet with a craving for more community involvement. In contrast to her actual situation, however, the imagined figure was unmarried and independent, living happily without a husband. This suggested Emily's desire for greater independence than she currently felt in her marriage.

Of her male figure, Emily said, "He's a semi-jock in cut-off shorts. He's muscular, about five feet eleven, with a hairy chest and curly hair on his head. He looks intent and sincere." She described him further as "earthy-looking" and as "pleasant, helpful, and cooperative." He appeared to have a mixture of the physical qualities she found attractive in men and the character traits that appealed to her in her husband.

On the Rorschach Test, Emily provided a total of 27 responses. The computer analysis identified three aspects of her responses as highly significant (see Appendix for details). First, anxiety, apprehension, and tension were found to be pervasive, based on her frequent use of the achromatic portions of the blot. Second, the overuse of shading in her form perceptions likewise was found to indicate significant anxiety as a result of excessive needs for affection. Third, a significantly exaggerated need for affectional response, along with a fear of rejection and a sense of the environment as anxiety-producing, was indicated through her frequent use of shading relative to a virtual lack of color responses.

Emily's Rorschach responses generally indicated a high level of creativity and involvement. Her relatively high form level of 82 percent also reflected a normal orientation toward her environment. The content of her perceptions, however, reflected her strong underlying sense of anxiety.

The theme of being helpless in the face of entrapment or engulfment was repetitive in her responses. On Card 1, for example, she saw a "spider" with "grippers," and on Card 4 she perceived a "monster" with "tentacles." Her perception in Card 5 was "an enemy . . . it's going to wrap itself around the victim," and on Card 10 she described "a helpless object with no arms to defend itself and no feet. . . . It's an innocent victim . . . in danger of being eaten."

Summary

Both her psychological tests and the material elicited through the unstructured interviews reflected the lively, cooperative aspects of Emily's character, as well as her apprehension that she would be trapped, abused, or hurt by her involvements with people. Her early family relationships, reinforced by her first marriage, made her view of relationships understandable. At the same time, she was drawn by the element of risk in relationships, was excited by fantasies of gentle rape, and wondered if excitement was possible in a stable relationship. In her first marriage she found both physical abuse and sexual excitement; in her second she had less objective basis for her fears, but they persisted nevertheless, and she needed sexual adventures to add excitement and risk to her marriage.

Marijuana had enabled her to tolerate the abuse of her first marriage. She used her "busyness" to escape from closeness and commitment in her present marriage and saw marijuana as helping her to tolerate the tension that resulted from having to keep busy. Marijuana also served more directly to assist her in reducing the tension she felt with her husband and children. She equated commitment and routine with death and entrapment, largely out of the experiences she had had while growing up and during her first marriage. For years she had felt dead and without a sense of identity and feared this would happen to her again. Her fantasy tickets seemed built into her current marriage to provide some protection against her fears. In a related vein, she was glad the sessions were coming to an end because she did not like the commitment of regular appointments.

She indicated on her questionnaire that marijuana improved her ability to be tolerant and understanding of others, and she felt she could deal with her children better when high. Yet it became evident that what she considered being understanding and more tolerant of others was actually a reflection of having emotionally removed herself from her family, which had more disturbing consequences than she was willing to admit.

Similarly, on her questionnaire responses she rated her life as satisfactory in virtually every respect. Yet it was clear that she experienced a good deal of frustration in key areas of life, and her description of things as about to become "absolutely tops" appeared to be more a statement of will or faith rather than a true reflection of what she actually felt.

Jeffrey Gordon

Screening Session and Questionnaire

Jeffrey Gordon was a short, slightly built, bearded man of thirty-five who had been divorced for almost four years from a woman with whom he had had an 11-year marriage. Although his former wife had legal custody of their three children—a daughter of three and two sons aged six and ten—since the separation the children had lived with him in a suburb of New York City. He currently earned a modest salary working as an assistant sales manager for a clothing manufacturer. Although he had been dating a woman in her early twenties for the last year, she had recently ended the relationship, and he described his life as lonely except for his interactions with the children.

Jeffrey had begun smoking marijuana at the age of fifteen and became a regular daily smoker about the age of twenty-one or twenty-two. For the past several years he had been smoking about five marijuana cigarettes a day. On days when he worked, most of his smoking took place while driving to and from his job and at home in the evening hours, whereas on non-working days he typically smoked throughout the day as well as at night. Although he saw marijuana as having the short-term effect of enhancing his ability to cope with his problems and to enjoy life more, he acknowledged on the questionnaire that it had an adverse effect on his memory, his ability to think clearly, and his long-term ability to solve the problems that faced him.

On the questionnaire he reported having frequent adverse reactions while smoking marijuana, particularly being "worried because I didn't know how people were reacting to me." He also said that while high he had frequently "seen myself as I really am and didn't like what I saw."

Out of a large list of different aspects of one's life, Jeffrey did not identify a single one as something he was "pleased" or "delighted" about. On the other hand, he indicated feeling "terrible" about his current sex life, the amount of intimacy, love, and warmth in his life, his degree of independence, and how much fun he was having in his life. He rated last year as a 2 on a questionnaire scale of 1 to 10 and the present year as a 1. Although he felt next year would be a 4, he indicated that for most people of his sex and age it would probably be a 5.

On the other questions he rated himself as "extremely" bothered recently by "feeling blue," "feeling tense and keyed up," "feeling self-conscious with others," and "feeling people will take advantage of you if you let them." He also indicated a very low level of self-esteem and said he had recently felt that he was close to having a nervous breakdown.

Interviews

Although his affective display in the interviews showed a good range, Jeffrey appeared to be mildly depressed and gave the impression of someone who found life's problems to be a great burden. During the sessions he was self-effacing, always compliant, overly cooperative, and looked for clues to what might be pleasing to the interviewer.

Jeffrey recognized that he allowed himself to be manipulated in relationships while remaining passive. During the course of his 11-year marriage he had been aware of his wife's having had several affairs, including one with his best friend, as well as attempting to have one with his brother. He reacted by feeling that he was doing something wrong and would ask himself how he might improve the relationship.

Despite a need to feel wanted and a great desire for affection, he did not enter into personal relationships without assurance of acceptance, remaining sensitive to rejection, unassertive, insecure, self-deprecatory, and consciously avoidant of areas of contention. As he described it, "I want an involvement, but I want it to come to me. If you enter the race, you can lose." In a recent relationship with a woman he had behaved in a compliant and unassertive manner, revealing little about his own needs and concentrating entirely on her problems and needs in an attempt to be pleasing and desired. After a year his passive style of interaction finally resulted in her ending the relationship.

At his job Jeffrey, although conscientious and capable, was unassertive and distant from others. He was dissatisfied with his inability to advance and stated that he allowed people to "dump" on him. In his last job, in which he had been the manager of several stores, he had worked seven days a week for little money during the first several months. "When I finally worked up the nerve to approach the boss," he said, "I let him snow me instead of standing up. Then I went home to my wife, who asked if I had spoken to the boss, and I said, 'Not yet. The timing's not right.' I was afraid to tell her, that she'd point out my weaknesses, and I knew them already." He then associated to his height. "Believe it or not, my height, or lack of height, bothers me a lot. I don't like being short. I equate that with stature. Short person, short stature."

Jeffrey was a giving, caring parent to his three children and appeared to have good relationships with them. He shopped, cooked, and cleaned the house himself. He spent time with the children every day, coming home directly from work to them, was concerned with their homework and their progress in school, and was demonstrably affectionate with them. His mother, who lived nearby, frequently baby-sat, but at times he hired a local teenager. He felt tremendously burdened by having the sole responsibility for parenting, and this weighed heavily on his mind. Although he felt his children were healthy and knew they could discuss their problems with him, he was often preoccupied by concerns about their development and worried about his ability to be "both mother and father" to them.

Jeffrey experienced guilt and anxiety at times about his feelings of resentment and fleeting thoughts of running away and escaping his responsibilities. Feeling the responsibility to his children, he recognized that "they didn't ask to be born." He added, "I was the product of a rather bad upbringing, a broken home, and a bad divorce. I don't know if I'm doing the best job that I can. I always feel I could be doing more."

In describing his own childhood he said, "I brought myself up. I had no parents that really cared. I do have a life of my own now, but I feel guilty about enjoying things. I feel I should forsake my own needs and desires for my kids. I have a defeatist attitude, a lack of confidence, feelings of general unworthiness."

He said that his ex-wife often told him to relax and enjoy things, but he explained that he did not know how to. He noted that, "It's been pointed out to me that I've cast myself in the role of victim; I'm always the victim. I hide, shut myself off." Fearful of taking a chance on people in relationships, he stated, "I rationalize that who would want me and my three kids. I never trusted my wife in 11 years of marriage. I find it difficult to trust people. Why does this person want me; what do they want from me?"

Jeffrey felt he did not know what happiness, peace, and contentment were. As he described it, "I find it difficult to accept praise or credit—or love for that matter. I find it difficult to believe people. I'm a survivor though, even if I don't like how I do it. My kids and I have survived the crises of the past years. Where is it going? When is it going to end? When can I enjoy things?" Jeffrey likened himself to a Saint Bernard. "A Saint Bernard," he said, "will adapt to any environment. Lock it in a closet and it'll adapt."

In talking of his history of marijuana smoking, Jeffrey gave "peer pressure" as the reason for his beginning to smoke at the age of fifteen. According to his description, "We were all friends for a couple of years before starting to smoke. They started first and turned me on. The first time I smoked was pure peer pressure. They had started pressuring me for several weekends. I gave in mainly to get them off my back."

He did not see his smoking marijuana as related to his desire to rebel against his parents because his father had already left home and his mother knew about his smoking shortly after he started. Her attitude had been "I can't fight it so I might as well go along with it."

He described his marijuana-smoking pattern before his marriage as light and sporadic, occurring primarily on weekends; he was, in his term, strictly a "party smoker." After he married, his smoking increased "because my wife was a regular marijuana user," although for a while it remained a social activity. Gradually, however, he found he had a growing need for marijuana, and over the course of a few years he began smoking on an increasingly heavy basis. At the time he was interviewed he was smoking four to six marijuana cigarettes in an average day, sometimes in the morning on the way to work, sometimes on his lunch break, usually on the way home from work, and always during the evening.

As he described it, marijuana did not make him feel more

social, explaining that he felt more self-conscious when high and more awkward. He did not regard marijuana as an escape but rather felt it allowed him "to deal with the same set of circumstances but on a diferent plane." Relatedly, he felt that marijuana helped him to deal with his loneliness, saying that after smoking, "I can space out and let my mind wander. The emphasis on the loneliness is less. It really doesn't lessen the pain; I just am able to deal with it on another level." In this respect he likened marijuana to aspirin in that it made the situation more bearable although it did not really get rid of the cause.

Jeffrey was the second of three sons raised in a suburban, middle-class Jewish family. His parents engaged in constant verbal and physical battles, and Jeffery recalled, "There was never any peace or harmony at home for as long as I remember." Each of his parents repeatedly threatened to leave and on occasion actually did so. He said he felt as though he had never had his mother or father at the same time, and he recalled numerous instances in which one of them would be threatening to walk out while he would be helplessly standing by, "begging and pleading."

When his parents engaged in loud arguments or became physically abusive, sometimes throwing lamps or other objects, Jeffrey experienced considerable fear and frequently attempted to be a mediator. Describing those times, he said, "It would kill me. I'd feel totally lost, total rejection. I didn't know what was happening. My whole security was shaken." Jeffrey described his older brother as staying out of their parents' difficulties, and his younger brother, he said, was too small to really know what was going on.

His earliest memory was of being in the basement of his house at the age of four fixing a blown fuse with his father. This memory appeared to incorporate both his anxiety about things going wrong at home and his wish to fix the situation with his father. For the most part, however, he viewed his parents as having been self-concerned and indifferent to him, and said he had always felt unloved, lonely, and unwanted. He became tearful in recounting, as an example of his mother's indifference to him, an incident in which he had been shot by a BB gun at the age of eight or nine. He ran home, and he remembered his older brother's concern and attempts to do something about the bleeding. His mother, who was getting dressed, came out and said, "I can't be bothered. I have an appointment at the beauty parlor." He reacted to such hurtful incidents by withholding his feelings, being obedient, compliant, and unassertive.

Jeffrey's tension and anxiety at home were further increased by his mother's frequent drunkenness. He said he often had had to clean up after her. He also described coming home one time and finding his typewriter smashed because she had wanted to type a letter and could not get it out of the "lock" position.

Jeffrey's parents' final separation occurred when he was thirteen years old after a battle on the day of his bar mitzvah. He and his brothers remained with their mother, who worked as a bookkeeper and secretary. His father often did not send money for child support but did pay for private school and later for some of Jeffrey's college tuition.

As an adolescent Jeffrey had friends but said he had never felt totally accepted by his group. Despite a yearning to be a part of things, he said, "I couldn't find a niche where I belonged." Although he dated through his adolescence, having intercourse for the first time at the age of thirteen, he always had only one girl at a time and felt he had never been a "swinger."

Feeling lost, with no direction, and no sense of belonging anywhere, he turned to his father for help at the age of fifteen and saw a psychologist for a year until "my father cut off the help." He added bitterly, "It took 11 months till the psychologist got anything out of me."

While Jeffrey was in college in the Midwest, majoring in philosophy, his younger brother, in talking to their father, "slipped that I had smoked pot." He complained that his father "didn't have the guts to call me directly" but instead communicated through his older brother that his financial support had been cut off. When Jeffrey called to talk to him about this, his father told him, "From now on you're not my son; I'm not your father," and then hung up. Jeffrey recalled that his first reaction was total fear, but soon after he decided he would make it on his own. He obtained some financial aid from school, and since that time he had had only a distant relationship with his father.

He described his relationship with his older brother as a "disaster." They had nothing to do with one another for a number of years until Jeffrey saw him on the occasion of their younger brother's wedding, which occurred only a few days after Jeffrey's divorce. They said only a few words to each other, but Jeffrey said the occasion put him in touch with the importance of family relationships, and he later wrote to his brother asking why there had to be such a lack of communication between them. The brother phoned Jeffrey the day he received the letter and subsequently came with his girlfriend to spend "a nice day" with Jeffrey and his children. They hugged when they left, but they had not spoken since that time.

Jeffrey said that his relationship with his younger brother had always been very good. When his younger brother ran away from home at the age of fourteen, he stayed with Jeffrey and his wife for a year, going to school in their neighborhood. He described his brother as "my best friend" and said he also had an excellet relationship with his brother's wife, calling her his sister. His brother and sister-in-law lived nearby with their mother, who in recent years had recovered from her previous alcoholism, and Jeffrey saw them at least once a week.

Jeffrey had married at the age of twenty-one while at home from college the summer after his junior year. One night he was with some of his old high school friends, and they went to pick up a friend who was working at an ice cream parlor. A girl poked her head into the car and said, "Oh, you're cute." It was not clear to whom she was referring, but the next day while Jeffrey was swimming with his friends the girl came over and "I felt a hand up and down my knee." He said he had assumed that they would simply "have fun for the summer," but 20 days later they were married. Although he said he knew he did not love her, she was attentive and giving and, in contrast to other girls he had gone out with, she did not seem to be "on the take."

He described his marriage as problematic right from the beginning in that he allowed his wife to dominate and "mother" him, while he took a very passive role. After the birth of their three children, she became bored with their relationship, began to attend less and less to her previously accepted responsibilities in the home and with the children, and began a series of affairs.

Jeffrey said he kept "mellow," largely through his increasing use of marijuana, and did not fully experience the reality of her behavior nor the anger he felt toward her. Although he said he had had fantasies of involvement with other women, he had been unable to bring himself to have a sexual relationship with anyone else.

He explained that he tried at all costs to avoid confrontations with his wife and worked to keep his feelings inside. He did this so successfully that he experienced her subsequent request for a divorce as totally unexpected and tried everything he could to convince her not to pursue it. In the divorce she obtained legal custody of the children with Jeffrey's acquiescence; she preferred not to keep them, however, and they had remained with him. Although he now felt that she was not a fit parent, he had done nothing to secure formal custody of the children.

In his relationships with women since the time of his divorce, he continued to experience the discomfort he had felt in his adolescence of dating more than one person at a time. He longed for a satisfying "one-on-one relationship" but kept himself away from social situations in which he might possibly meet someone with whom he would feel comfortable.

When Jeffrey was seen for three follow-up sessions approximately two years later, he looked well and was a little heavier. In response to being asked what had occurred in the interim he stated, "Many changes. The biggest is I got married."

In describing how he had met his wife, Angela, Jeffrey explained that she had been a neighbor of his for some time but they had never met. Her only child, a twelve-year-old son, was friends with his oldest son. She and Jeffrey had spoken on the phone several times, and she had invited him on several occasions to her home for a drink. Jeffrey said he had told her he would come by if he could work it out but had never done so. About a year ago Angela, who was a nursing supervisor at a nearby community hospital, finally invited him to a social function; he accepted, and that began the relationship.

Angela came from an Italian Catholic family and had been divorced for several years. She was the same age as Jeffrey and had also had a very bitter divorce. Jeffrey described her as having perviously dedicated her life to her work and to her son, but he said she now intended to leave administration and return to a less pressured nursing position.

He described Angela as "a good person, sensitive, caring, attentive; everything a Jewish wife isn't." Although he felt she was basically very shy, he said she was charming and generally marvelous with people. He gave as an example a recent trade show of his at which she had "reorganized the whole thing" and had made it a social success as well.

Jeffrey said that he and his new wife complemented each other very well. She, for example, had difficulty communicating what was really bothering her, whereas he felt he was able to be more open. She, on the other hand, helped him in social situations through her greater ability to cover up her shyness and interact with people. She also supported him in such household matters as paying the bills and was generous in giving him time to relax at the end of the day.

When asked what conflicts did exist, he responded, "Smoking reefer. That is the underlying conflict." He went on to explain that Angela's ex-husband had smoked marijuana heavily and had used it to "go off into his own world," leaving her alone. In addition to equating marijuana with her ex-husband, he said she was "deathly afraid" of a potential legal conflict and of its possible influence on the children. Jeffrey said he could understand her point with regard to the effects of marijuana on young people because as a nurse she had seen so many drug-related problems. In order not to upset her, he had stopped smoking in front of the children.

This had resulted in a marked change in Jeffrey's marijuana-smoking patterns, which were now centered primarily on the time when he was alone in the car driving to and from work. He said that although at times he would have liked to smoke at home, particularly on the weekends, he felt the "trade-off" was definitely worth it.

Jeffrey related that his children got along well with Angela's son although they did fight once in a while. His wife's son had a strained relationship with his father, whom he saw about once a month, but related very well to Jeffrey and was "very accepting" of his mother's new life. Angela had said that for all practical purposes Jeffrey was her son's father.

Jeffrey described his children as getting along with Angela "better than with their own mother" and added, "She doesn't have to tell them that she loves them, they know it." He expressed some concern about his oldest son, who was almost thirteen and whom he described as "nervous, high strung, and consistently worrying that we're going to break up." Saying he saw a lot of himself in this son, he noted that the boy did not have many friends, held in his feelings, and was prone to peer pressure. He also had been having difficulties in his school work for the first time and had recently been suspended for cutting school after some other students called him "chicken" and dared him to do it.

Although concerned about his son and having one more child to deal with, Jeffrey said that he felt calmer and more tranquil. The difference was that now "I have someone to do it with; I'm not alone anymore. The pressures are different because we can feed off of each other."

Although describing himself as more receptive to people, less anxious, and less depressed than he had been in years, Jeffrey said that he could not describe himself as a happy person and continued to have occasional downs. Much of this appeared to be focused around work. Although he was currently making a little more money which, together with his wife's salary, had allowed them to save quite a bit toward a home, his company had merged with another, and in the process Jeffrey lost much of the authority he previously had. As he put it, "I went from middle management to an Indian."

Although he described himself as "not as fearful as I used to be," he said he continued to feel that "if I open my mouth [at work] it'll only make for an uncomfortable atmosphere," and that sometimes "the paranoid fear is still there that I'll be fired." As a result he had done nothing to assert himself in an effort to regain a greater measure of responsibility in his job.

Recently his manager had been fired, and his wife had encouraged him to go after the positon. Jeffrey was ambivalent, feeling that the job had a lot of pressure as well as longer hours. He was shortly thereafter called in by his boss who was clearly considering Jeffrey for the promotion. The boss noted that Jeffrey had never taken any initiative to get a higher position and had never asked for a raise. Jeffrey responded by talking about his "fear of success," and someone else got the job. When confronted in the interview with the fact that he had destroyed his chances, he admitted that he had not wanted the job. When asked about his feelings about not getting ahead, he went into a long discussion about the problems of this particular job and rationalized that there are "other ways to get ahead." Later he conceded that he still had a fear of responsibility and authority and that he did not react well under pressure.

Jeffrey recognized that these fears and his related passivity were holding him back from achieving his potential. He described himself as often feeling angry about his passivity, and he knew he paid a high price for it with respect to not getting ahead.

Although marijuana was not the cause of his passivity, he agreed that it played a large role in helping him to tolerate difficult situations rather than making any real changes. At the close of the interviews, when it was suggested to him that he think seriously about this, he characteristically stated that indeed he would and that change would be easier because he now had a good wife behind him.

Psychological Tests

During the test session Jeffrey was alert and efficient in his responses but appeared to put a good deal of pressure on himself and was frequently self-critical. On the WAIS-R he obtained a Full Scale IQ of 108, falling within the average range of functioning. The 20-point discrepancy between his Verbal IQ of 118 and his Performance IQ of 98, suggestive of a strong preference for thought rather than action, was found to be highly significant (Naglieri, 1982) and likely to occur among fewer than 15 percent of persons in Jeffrey's age range (Knight, 1983).

Jeffery's subtest scores on the WAIS-R were as follows:

Verbal IQ = 118 (Bright Normal)		*Performance IQ = 98 (Average)*	
Information	13	Picture Completion	11
Digit Span	13	Picture Arrangement	12

Vocabulary	14	Block Design	10
Arithmetic	12	Object Assembly	8
Comprehension	13	Digit Symbol	8
Similarities	13		

Jeffrey's strongest abilities were found in the area of general knowledge and verbal fluency; he was weakest in speed, accuracy, and visual-motor coordination. Difficulties were observed in particular in his work with numbers. He responded, for example, that the temperature at which water boiled was 210°C and that there were five billion people living in the United States.

Performance scores showed that he was best in Picture Arrangement, indicative of a fairly good understanding of others. His low scores in Object Assembly and Digit Symbol, however, pointed to difficulties in visual-motor organization.

The MMPI report provided the following outline of Jeffrey's personality: "This subject seems to be a person who has difficulty maintaining controls over his impulses. When he behaves in a socially unacceptable manner, he is likely to experience guilt and distress, although his concern may reflect situational difficulties rather than an expression of internal conflicts. His behavior shows a self-defeating and self-punitive tendency. At the present time he seems to be depressed, restless, and somewhat agitated. He is distressed about his failure to achieve goals and pessimistic about the future. He is a rigid person who may react to anxiety with phobias, compulsions, or obsessive rumination. Chronic tension and excessive worry are common. He appears to be an idealistic, inner-directed person who may be seen as quite socially perceptive and sensitive to interpersonal interactions. However, he may be hesitant to become involved in social relationships. He is sensitive, reserved, and somewhat uncomfortable, especially in new and unfamiliar situations."

On the Draw-A-Person Test, Jeffrey first produced a somewhat fearful-looking male figure (Figure 5). Emphasis on the ears suggested a hypervigilance regarding what others said about him. The female figure was drawn in profile, suggesting

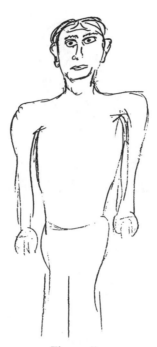

Figure 5.

evasiveness and defenses against fullness of contact with others. He had difficulty with the breast line of the female and over-looked her waist, indicative of anxieties related to his feelings toward women. The feet of the female lacked substance, and those of the male were cut off the page entirely, reflecting a lack of autonomy on Jeffrey's part and difficulties in standing on his own feet. The sparsely drawn hands seen in both figures were further felt to be a projection of Jeffrey's feelings of inadequacy.

He described the male figure as follows: "He's definitely deformed. He's twenty-six or twenty-seven, of average height and build. He's an average guy, getting through. He's out of proportion. The shoulders are too wide for his body; his arms are too short; long-waisted; very rigid. He's standing, staring off into space.

"He's single, with no family or commitments. He's lonely but adjusting, making the best of it. He works as a cab driver. He

Figure 6.

sees a lot of things, but he doesn't like it as he's going nowhere. He's drifting, thinking where he's going, what he wants. He keeps a low profile, doesn't bother anybody, and keeps himself open to experience. Eventually, well, he'll survive." Jeffrey commented that there was a lot of himself in his story.

His description of the female figure (Figure 6) reflected similar themes of loneliness and uncertainty regarding the future: "She's nobody in particular. She's in her twenties, single and unattached. She's looking for the ideal: career and marriage. She's a nurse who is anxious but patient about her future. Concerned about the unknown, she fears that she'll meet somebody and things won't be right. Eventually, she gets married and gives up her career but winds up getting divorced. She regrets having given up her career. She becomes lonely and gets married again. Same cycle repeats. She returns to work and winds up a spinster and a career woman."

The computer analysis of the 18 responses that Jeffrey provided to the Rorschach identified two aspects as highly significant (see Appendix for details). First, his high number of whole responses (nine) compared to only two human movement responses indicated that his productive resources were too low to match his aspirations. Second, he was found to have significant anxiety over his strong needs for affection, based on the use of shading in his form perceptions.

Based on 11 good, 6 adequate, and 1 minus response, Jeffrey's level equalled 78 percent. His good form level combined with his six popular responses indicated fairly good contact with reality. Overall, his responses suggested feelings of vulnerability and inadequacy, and images reflecting impaired self-image were pervasive: a bat with "misshapen claws" (Card 1); a "squashed bug" (Card 4); a butterfly with "torn wings" (Card 5); and a "squashed spider" (Card 10). That the damage to his self-esteem was related to frustration of his needs for care and affection was suggested by such responses as his elaboration of the torn wings of the bat as the result of "fighting over food."

Summary

In Jeffrey's case the questionnaire data, the results of psychological testing, and the material obtained through the interviews provided a strongly consistent picture. His questionnaire responses reflected a recognition that marijuana enhanced his ability to cope with problems in the short run but adversely affected his long-term ability to solve them. His description of his drawing of a man was of a deformed but average guy, lonely but making the best of it, drifting but getting through, keeping a low profile, not bothering anybody, and eventually surviving. His self-critical attitude, depressed mood, and general discontent with life were clearly reflected in this description. His drawing of a female also revealed a depressive theme of loneliness as well as fears of being hurt, with consequent withdrawal from others. The 20-point discrepancy between his Verbal and Performance scores on the WAIS-R further pointed to diminished activity and accomplishment and suggested frustration.

The Rorschach report also was generally very consistent

with the clinical picture, revealing feelings of weakness (particularly as a result of unmet affectional needs), feelings of helplessness in which forces outside of the self control one's fate, depressive feelings, feelings of alienation, hostile feelings toward authority, feelings of inadequacy despite efforts to keep his life together, a lack of trust of others, and a tendency to be overcautious and overly controlled in his relationships.

Jeffrey was a product of a home filled with tension, where he had lived with the insecurity of never knowing when one of his parents might abandon him. In adult life he continued the pattern he established early in his youth of avoiding all disharmony. He continued to pay the price of loneliness, low self-esteem, and depression for his inordinate needs for affection and acceptance, which coexisted with a hypersensitivity to rejection. His need to avoid self-assertion and the expression of anger led him to feel impotent. He was a "short" emasculated man who felt inadequate in life.

He derived some comfort from his image of himself as a survivor, likening himself to a Saint Bernard dog that can adapt to the most difficult surroundings. From the net result of his efforts, however, he derived little pleasure or satisfaction.

For Jeffrey marijuana served the purpose of decreasing his feelings of loneliness and isolation. He likened marijuana to aspirin in that it deadened the pain but did not remove the cause. Being high on marijuana did not improve his self-image or his confidence socially, but he felt it helped him to forget his troubles.

What was further elaborated through the clinical sessions was how marijuana reinforced Jeffery's ability to remain passively tied to situations in which he was poorly treated. In his relationship with his first wife it enhanced his ability to avoid both dealing with her infidelity and being in touch with his own anger. Similarly, smoking marijuana on the way to work and on his way home enhanced his capacity to avoid self-assertion and to avoid thinking about his frustration and lack of fulfillment.

ELLEN THORNTON

Screening Session and Questionnaire

Ellen Thornton was an attractive thirty-eight-year-old woman who for the past seven years had been working as a freelance writer. She had published several books and a variety of articles dealing primarily with social issues. She had been divorced for the past 10 years. She had no children and currently shared an apartment with a roommate. Ellen first tried marijuana at the age of twenty-three and did not become a regular daily user until she was twenty-eight. She currently smoked about 2½ marijuana cigarettes a day, a little less when she was heavily involved in a writing project and often considerably more on weekends. On the questionnaire she indicated that her primary reasons for using marijuana were to relax and relieve tension; for fun, kicks, and excitement; and to enhance her sexual interest and pleasure. She felt that the drug had a negative effect on her memory and her ability to concentrate and think clearly, but otherwise she saw it as enhancing her ability to avoid boredom and to enjoy her life.

Overall, her questionnaire responses indicated high self-esteem and a fairly high level of satisfaction with most aspects of her life at the present time. She characterized herself as only "somewhat satisfied" with her single life-style, however, and said that she felt "terrible" about the lack of job security she had. Although she rated the previous year as a 2 on a scale of 1 to 10, she felt her present situation was an 8 ("Actually quite good"). She was unable to project what the next year might be.

Interviews

Ellen was cheerful, friendly, and open in manner during the interviews and seemed to enjoy talking about herself. She considered that until 10 years ago her life had followed a fairly traditional course: a happy childhood and adolescence, college, and marriage. At the age of twenty-eight, however, she ended her marriage and moved to Colorado. She began heavy, daily marijuana smoking about that time and felt this had had something to do with a rebellion against her previous way of life.

After graduating from college, Ellen lived in Europe for a while, and during that period she met a man who was stationed there in the army. Several months later she married him. She described him as handsome, bright, sociable, and athletic, and although in retrospect she did not think that she was in love with him, she felt he was "acceptable" and added that "marriage was then in."

After he completed his army tour they returned to the United States, where he enrolled in college to finish his undergraduate degree and was then accepted at a medical school abroad. For the next two years while he studied, Ellen taught English at a nearby high school.

Initially, she attributed the breakup of their marriage to the "stirrings of feminism," saying, "I didn't want to be another person's appendage. I wasn't quite sure about my own identity and wondered if I really wanted to be a doctor's wife." She said she did not like the idea of being tied down to one location because of the practice her husband would be establishing and was reluctant to give up her travels.

As she talked further, however, it became clear that there were things about her husband that she disliked and did not respect. She considered him to be an angry, unkind, and at times abusive person. She related how he would curse at her when they were skiing because she could not ski as well as he wished.

During the early months of their marriage, while still living in Europe, Ellen and her husband agreed not to have a child so she would be free to support him when he started back to school. When she became pregnant shortly thereafter, they both decided she should get an abortion. Ellen, however, described his attitude as totally unsupportive emotionally. He refused to ask for a leave to accompany her to Austria, where she tried unsuccessfully to have the abortion. Finally, she returned to the United States to have it. At that time abortions were still illegal in this country, and the experience was extremely unpleasant. When she rejoined her husband in Europe, she said he expressed no concern for her, merely asking her coldly whether it had been a boy or girl.

Shortly before Ellen left her husband, her mother died. As she described it, "My mother was a good person, and I didn't want to do things to disappoint her. I think that her death kind of freed me psychologically, so then I could leave my husband."

After the breakup of her marriage, she traveled for a while with a female friend. This woman, who was several years younger than Ellen, smoked marijuana, and Ellen also began to smoke occasionally during this period.

Some months later, she returned to the United States and enrolled in graduate school in Boston and spent time with her father and sisters who lived there. During this period she was involved in an incident that she said "really threw me." One night as she was leaving the school where she was studying, a young man approached her in the parking lot and asked her for a lift to a garage, saying he had run out of gas. At the garage he was joined by two other men who took Ellen at knife point to a deserted area, robbed her, and raped her several times. She described herself as terrified, not knowing from one second to the next what would happen. She said that the men kept telling her they were going to kill her and added, "I had every reason in the world to believe them."

For a week she did not tell anyone about the experience or report it to the police. Her attackers were apprehended following another rape a short time later, however, and her testimony resulted in the conviction of one of them. The other two had plea-bargained and as a result did not come to trial.

Ellen said she was depressed and frightened for a long time after the rape, particularly when walking in the streets. She was angry at herself for being gullible in believing the first man's story about the gas and for being too frighened to scream. Although she did not dream about the incident itself, she had frequent nightmares about being in threatening and dangerous situations. She did not seek out counseling or therapy, dealing with her feelings instead by beginning to write a book about her experience.

Ellen said she had come to Boston to start a new life, but the rape made her want to start it elsewhere. Feeling that she did not want her reaction to this experience to force her to leave precipitously, however, she completed the semester at school and then moved to Colorado. She said she was drawn to that area because she had friends there. She added that she had also wanted to get far away from Boston.

After settling in Colorado she became involved with a man whom she described as gentle, funny, and somewhat offbeat. He worked in a bicycle store, but she said that in those days it did not matter to her what someone did for a living. She said she felt that he loved her, but she was too upset in the aftermath of the rape to give him much in return, and she realized how much she cared for him only after he became tired of "putting love in a sieve" and left her. This man was a regular marijuana smoker, and while with him she began to smoke regularly and heavily, saying that it helped her to deal with the mixture of tension and depression she felt during this period.

She described her first several years in Colorado as a healing period. She completed her book on rape and began lecturing on the topic before various women's groups. During this period she also wrote extensively about bisexuality and teenage pregnancy.

While writing on bisexuality she went to bed once with the woman who had suggested the topic to her. Subsequently, she became sexually involved on single occasions with two other women, both times following evenings of using cocaine and Quaaludes. In speaking of these experiences, she said that although in recent years she had had no real desire for involvement with a woman, she wished society made no distinction between heterosexual and homosexual.

After being in Colorado for several years she became involved with a wealthy businessman who always had cocaine available. She was then sharing an apartment with a rock musician; the people he associated with always had it around as well, and for a brief period Ellen also became heavily involved with cocaine. She saw her use of "coke" as giving her a feeling of control and a sense that she could do "everything and anything." It also stimulated conversation, she felt, and allowed her to come to know people in ways she did not otherwise do. Ultimately, she decided to stop cocaine because she did not like the idea that it was beginning to control her life.

She had returned East two years prior to the interviews, in

order to get away from her involvement with cocaine, to further her writing, and to be near a man she had recently met who was moving to New York. He had his own business and seemed to Ellen to be bright, competent, and able to deal with life. Only after she had become involved with him and they were living together did she learn that he had been a heroin addict.

Within three or four months he resumed using heroin on a daily basis and Ellen decided to try it too, perhaps, she thought, to prove she cared for her boyfriend. At first she said it made her sick, but after a few times it gave her a warm, enveloping feeling of comfort that shut out the rest of the world unlike any other drug she had used. Sometimes she would take it with cocaine and would be high and sociable for a while and then would then settle into "a quiet high" that did not involve other people. She said that she became worried when she really began to enjoy heroin, and as a consequence she gave it up, finally leaving the relationship. She subsequently wrote an article about her experiences with this man, and she described the success of that piece as a "breakthrough" for her freelance writing.

Ellen said that a few months before our interviews the heroin user had called her for the first time in more than a year. She had seen him several times and had slept with him. Noting that he had been impotent toward the end of their earlier relationship, Ellen felt he had wanted to prove to her that he could now function sexually.

During the time she was being interviewed she became sexually involved with a married man who was a successful executive. Although they saw each other several times a week, neither of them, she said, wanted a full-time, exclusive relationship. However, she enjoyed the fact that with him she felt stimulated intellectually and was able to share many of her interests which had not been the case with her heroin-using friend. She was also sharing her apartment with a male roommate. Although she described her relationship with him as affectionate but platonic, she considered him "one of the men in my life."

In discussing these relationships Ellen noted that she had always had a problem getting angry with people in general and particularly with men who did not treat her well. She felt this had been an issue with her former husband and with the wealthy businessman with whom she had been involved in Colorado. She wondered if there were something masochistic about the way she had stayed in those relationships.

She described herself as someone who liked to make decisions in a spontaneous, sometimes "insane" way. As she put it, "I seem to need a dose of spontaneity in my life to keep me going. I seem to get bored quite easily." She gave as an example an incident that had happened one morning while she was living in Colorado: "It was raining in Denver, and I said, 'I can't handle this—I'm going to Mexico.' So in the afternoon I flew to Mexico." She added, "I haven't done that as much lately." She gave as another example of living spontaneously that if she had plans to go to a party or a social event and could not find a parking space nearby, she often would decide to skip it, whereas finding a space was a favorable omen that would lead her to go.

She believed very much in astrology, and although she said she did not base her life on it, she used it as a guide in her relationships. As she described it, "I would never get sexually involved with a Capricorn. They are diametrically opposed to Cancer [her sign], and Capricorn is too serious and too heavy a sign." She also believes in past and future lives, which she said kept her from being "devastated" if something she wanted did not happen, "because it could happen in another lifetime and probably will."

In speaking of her marijuana smoking, Ellen noted that over the past ten years, during which she had smoked on a daily basis, she had "survived" as a freelance writer because she had maintained "a strict dichotomy between my work hours and my relaxation hours." She said she definitely did not feel that any drug would enhance her writing ability, adding that she had experimented with writing after smoking marijuana and had found that "I don't come out with anything profound."

She came back to the subject of marijuana and its relation to her work in a subsequent interview saying, "I said the other day that I didn't use marijuana in a creative sense, but in a way that's not completely accurate. There are days when I'm sitting there looking at a blank piece of paper and nothing is happening. And I will find that if I smoke a small amount of grass, that will at least get me going, so there will be something on the paper, if only a few salvageable sentences or paragraphs." She also noted, "At night when I am high sometimes a phrase will come to mind that I'll jot down—the title for one of my books came to me after having several joints one evening."

Mostly, she said, she smoked to lighten things up and because of the silliness it permitted her. Ellen noted that, especially when smoking with her friends, "it helps me change my focus. Things will seem ridiculous or funny that wouldn't if I were looking at them completely straight." She went on to say, "Sometimes I feel I do drugs out of boredom. It's something to do. It alters reality just a tiny bit, sometimes not even as much as I would like it to. I've stuck mainly to marijuana because of the price factor and because I don't think it does the long-range damage that something like coke could possibly do to a person's system."

Describing marijuana as a major part of her social relationships with her friends, she noted, "I wonder if I should find more creative uses of my leisure time, but it's not as if I'm a blundering idiot or walking into walls or anything, because grass doesn't affect me that way. Yet I was mildly horrified when I was asked [during her screening interview] for an estimate of how much I smoked, to think I smoke three joints during an evening and more on weekends."

Ellen spent most of her growing-up years in a Boston suburb. Her father was a professor of European history, and because of his leaves and sabbaticals they traveled a good deal. For various periods during Ellen's adolescence the family lived in Europe.

Ellen was the middle of three daughters. She said that as a teenager she had felt closer to her older sister because they did a lot of things together. In later years, however, she felt she had become closer to and had more in common with her younger sister. Her older sister had a responsible administrative position and had never married. Ellen described her as a "dominant, manipulative, controlling, and dynamic person." Her younger sister, on the other hand, had been married for many years without having children and had recently been divorced.

In speaking of her childhood Ellen said that all three daughters had always known they were loved. She emphasized that the family had had many traditions that bound them to-gether, that the children were trusted, and that they were not spanked.

She had a great deal of difficulty, however, in giving a pic-ture of her parents and particularly of her mother. She said she had never thought about what they were like, adding, "Maybe I didn't want to look." She recalled her parents as having been af-fectionate with each other and said she had never seen them fight. Although saying that her father was respected by the chil-dren, she noted that it was their mother whom they had liked.

In elaborating this, Ellen said, "There's a certain tone of voice and a certain look that our father had and still has to this day, that you know you have messed up." She went on to say that she had always tried not to give him anything to disapprove of. All of the girls, she said, did well in school, which was important to him, but unlike her older sister, she and her younger sister tended to be secretive and to avoid open fights with their par-ents.

In spite of her attempts at compliance, Ellen felt her father had always preferred both of her sisters to her but repeatedly said that she had never resented this. On the other hand, she de-scribed herself as having been the closest of the three girls to her mother, whom she saw as self-sacrificing and always there for her. She felt unsure, however, about how her mother had really felt about her life and regretted that she had never asked her.

One of Ellen's clearest memories of growing up was of a time she went to camp at the age of fifteen. She recalled the enormous sense of exhilaration she discovered at not being known as anyone's sister or daughter. She felt she had finally found a sense of identity of her own. She had made a similar point with regard to leaving her husband, which led the inter-viewer to question what it was that made it hard for her to feel confident about who or what she was. She attributed it to being a middle child and to her father's preference for the other two girls.

Ellen described having had a recurrent dream throughout her childhood in which she was an Indian woman on horseback and part of a group that was attacking white settlers. The dream suggested an image of herself as an outsider, and when this was shared with her, it appeared to have an impact on her. Her initial reaction, however, was to say that it spoiled the fun of her own interpretation, that she had been an Indian in a previous life. In the process of discussing this dream, she mentioned that she had received a call from her drug-abusing friend who was back on heroin and had had himself hospitalized. This led the interviewer to question whether she felt a strong attraction to outsiders or, as it were, to other "Indians." She agreed this was the case.

She also was asked about the discrepancy between the dream image of herself as an attacking Indian and the picture she had given of herself as someone who had always had trouble being angry with people. She pointed out that although she would be carrying a tomahawk in a meancing way, there was never any blood in the dream. She wondered if the settlers might have represented her family and agreed that if this indeed were so, it suggested that not only did she not identify with them but had repressed a good deal of anger toward them as well. She also agreed that the fact that the Indians had been the unintended victims of the white settlers, who could find no place for them, was to some degree parallel to her sense of herself and her family situation. She then made the point with regard to her upcoming psychological testing that she was not sure she wanted to learn more about herself and observed that she probably had never gone into therapy because she had not wanted to look at herself and her life so closely.

Ellen came back to the Indian dream in a later session, stating that she had discussed it with her younger sister. In their conversation, she said, they had discussed the fact that none of the three sisters had children and wondered whether that had something to do with how they had felt growing up in their family.

In the course of the sessions Ellen also related a dream she had had shortly before starting the interviews. She was staring out of the window of the house of some friends who lived on a bay. A boat came into the bay and stirred up a large wave that came up to the window, but the glass held and did not break. The dream suggested both the turbulence that threatened her as well as the danger of looking too hard or too closely at her life.

Marijuana seemed to help her keep the turbulence under control, while allowing her to avoid the close scrutinizing of herself that she feared.

When she was seen 15 months later, Ellen had become seriously involved with the married executive with whom she had been going out and was now seeing him five times a week. She felt she was in love with him and he with her, and she hoped that they would eventually get married. She described him as gentle, warm, supportive, bright, and funny, and added that she had never had a better sexual relationship with anyone. In response to a direct question she said she did not believe that their feelings for each other would change if he were to become available.

She had continued to maintain her friendships with all of the past men and women in her life (except for her former husband), including the man who had worked in the bicycle store in Colorado, the man who had been addicted to heroin, and the man whom she had until recently shared her apartment, who was planning to get married. She said, however, she had no desire for involvement with anyone else since her current relationship had developed.

She reported that she had stopped smoking cigarettes since her earlier interviews and that her use of marijuana was now restricted to occasional social occasions. She added that she no longer kept any marijuana in her house. In explaining what had led to these changes, she said that she had felt that it was time to get her life together. She went on to say that her current lover did not smoke either tobacco or marijuana and that she had stopped her cigarette habit as a birthday present to him. In addition, she said, smoking tobacco was a messy, smelly, unhealthy habit and that marijuana also was probably unhealthy. Since she had previously said that she used marijuana to relax and to relieve her boredom, she was asked what she did now that she was not using marijuana. She laughingly replied, "For one thing, I'm having more fun in bed."

This precipitated a discussion of the relationship of her drug use to the men she was and had been involved with. It was pointed out that she had first become heavily involved with marijuana at a time when she was involved with a man who smoked heavily. Although her marijuana use had persisted, when she had been involved with a man who used cocaine she started using that drug as well, and a similar pattern had occurred with her friend who used heroin. Now she was involved with someone who did not smoke cigarettes or marijuana, and she had stopped one and cut down the others. She reacted to this with some discomfort, saying that she did not like to think that the men in her life had that degree of influence on her. Rather, the satisfaction she received in her current relationship seemed to her to be the most important factor in diminishing her need for drugs.

During the course of the follow-up sessions the interviewer read Ellen's book on rape and an article she had written about her heroin-using friend, and these were discussed with her. In response to the interviewer's comment that in her book she had written movingly of rapes involving other women without detailing her own experience, and in the article she had discussed her affair with the heroin user without indicating her own involvement with heroin, Ellen agreed that she only partly revealed herself in what she wrote. She said that earlier drafts of the rape book had been more filled with her anger toward men but that editors were less interested in that.

She indicated that since she had stopped smoking she had been having unpleasant dreams perhaps once a month. She said she had dreamed she was walking on a deserted street in the city, and a man came out of a park in a threatening way as though he were going to attack her. She noted that this dream and the others always ended at this point, and that often in such deams she wanted to scream but was unable to.

Although she described the dreams as very similar to those she had had after her rape, she connected her current dreams with the fact that where she currently lived she had to walk on dark streets at night. In discussing the dreams, however, she associated to her rape experience, saying that she had not been able to scream that night and subsequently felt that was an important part of a woman's attempt to protect herself. In spite of the fact that she had changed in significant ways since that time and certainly was much less gullible and submissive, her dreams suggested that she was not totally over the trauma of the rape. She agreed she was not and added that she did not think she ever would be completely.

Discussion of another recent dream in which her former

husband was carrying a four- or five-year-old child into a men's room led to Ellen's saying that she had been thinking in recent months about children. She expressed considerable ambivalence about having a child, saying she did not think she could become pregnant and that she did not take precautions to prevent pregnancy. Were she to become pregnant, however, she said she would be glad and would keep the child despite the circumstances. She wondered if that would be a way of bringing her current relationship to a point where a decision would have to be made.

This led her to reveal that she and her married lover had spoken of setting a time limit for deciding where their relationship was going and that they both had agreed that not to do so would be unfair to everyone involved. Although acknowledging that there was the potential for lots of difficult feelings ahead, she claimed not to be worried about the future, saying that "time just sort of goes on."

Psychological Tests

Ellen was friendly and open during the testing, and although she talked in an almost compulsive fashion, her intelligence was apparent in her conversation. Though previously married, she described herself to the tester as "single," suggesting a decisiveness to her break with her former married life.

On the WAIS-R Ellen's Full Scale IQ was found to be 120 based on a Verbal IQ of 122 and a Performance IQ of 111. This placed her in the superior range of functioning. Although the 11-point discrepancy between her Verbal and Performance scores was not found to be highly significant (Naglieri, 1982), her subtest profile, presented below, showed an unusually high degree of variability, thought to be suggestive of anxiety.

Verbal IQ = 122 (Superior)		*Performance IQ = 111 (Bright Normal)*	
Information	16	Picture Completion	12
Digit Span	6	Picture Arrangement	8
Vocabulary	17	Block Design	12

Arithmetic	12	Object Assembly	8
Comprehension	15	Digit Symbol	14
Similarities	13		

Ellen's verbal organization and expression were superior, and she had an outstanding range of information. Her lowest score, in Digit Span, appeared to be the result of intentional non-participation. During this part of the test she noted that she hated to memorize, especially numbers. Her attitude suggested a strong preference for spontaneity and a resistance to being constricted. In the Performance area, her low score in Picture Arrangement suggested poor empathetic ability in sizing up social situations. Her other low Performance score was in Object Assembly, revealing difficulties in visual organization.

The MMPI provided the following conclusions: "The validity of this subject's test results has been impaired by a strong tendency to deny problems and to present herself in a favorable light. She appears to be a sensitive, modest, and somewhat overly feminine person. This may express itself in an almost masochistic willingness to assume burdens and to place herself in situations in which she will be imposed upon. She may have problems centering around hostility and resentment toward members of her family. To the extent that she controls the direct expression of these feelings, she may be a bitter, resentful, and perhaps somewhat irresponsible person. Where control factors are not present, however, the hostility may be expressed in direct antisocial behavior. In any event, she is likely to have problems in establishing close personal relationships."

The figures (Figures 7 and 8) Ellen produced on the Draw-A-Person Test were qualitatively good but noteworthy for their amorphous line quality, an index of fairly significant anxiety and/or uncertain ego boundaries. The female figure's head was not attached to the partially drawn neck, suggesting a split between what the head knows and what the body does. The lower legs and feet also were missing, and Ellen herself pointed out that "the torso is on backward," a comment which suggested that she experienced distortions in her self-view. The unisex clothing on the female was thought to suggest a problem in feminine identity—the emphasized femininity in the figure's face was

Figure 7.

considered more apparent than real—and the hands conveyed feelings of inadequacy.

Ellen's story about the woman she drew had a quality that might be expected from a professional writer: "This is supposed to be my friend. She is off on an adventure, a trip to Tahiti, which would serve a couple of purposes. She wants to go to Tahiti to relax, to meet some new people, and not to deal with the hustle and bustle of everyday life. In Tahiti it would be pre-arranged for her to meet someone—a male or female. The companionship and the sharing of experiences makes the experience more wonderful. Things go all right; the sun does shine. Her spirits pick up and she feels fine, physically and emotionally. There's always the return to reality but with that extra wonderful feeling."

Ellen's male figure was remarkably similar to the female in its posture, pose, and position on the page. Like the woman, the

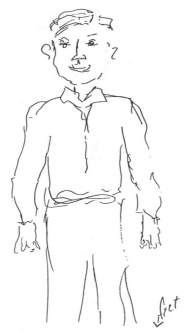

Figure 8.

man's head was disconnected from the body, the lower legs and feet were missing, and the hands were inadequately drawn.

She described the man she drew as follows: "He's a fairly chipper individual, not at all concerned that he has no feet. He has hair on top of his head. He's youthful in outlook and perspective but older in years—he's about forty. He has no facial hair. He's not too tall, five feet eight or shorter. I'm more attracted to men on my eye level. He's also inquisitive, with a good sense of humor, and there's a twinkle in the eye. He lives alone comfortably, in a four-room apartment, with lots of books, a little bit of clutter, and the usual complement of electronic equipment—a TV and stereo. He's more interested in literature than music; throw in a couple of plants and a pet—a cat rather than a dog. He's involved with a core of solid relationships and, beyond that, acquaintances of a professional and private nature. He works in the media, print media, as a journalist rather than an editor. Right now he's working on a particular assignment: covering a story on the probable alternatives to sending flowers, such as balloons, candy, grass, etc.; who's doing it and whether this can be made into a viable occupation. The end result is an amusing, entertaining, an informative article."

Although both stories reflected a high degree of self-identification, more of Ellen appeared to be revealed in her description of the man she had drawn than in her story about the woman. Also evident were several attempts to soften male–female differences through such comments as the fact that the man had "no facial hair," was at her eye level, and had interests centered around the home.

Ellen provided a total of 17 responses to the Rorschach cards. Identified as highly significant through the computer analysis (see Appendix for details) was her creative intelligence, reflected in her much greater than average number of whole responses (14). At the same time, her fewer than average number of detail responses (3) pointed to emotional disturbance, and her overuse of shading in her form perceptions was found to be indicative of excessive needs for affection.

Although Ellen's form level of 80 percent indicated secure ties to reality, her small number of popular responses (3) indicated that she did not have a strong need to be conventional. Frequently noted in her responses was the use of humor and playfulness to deal with pain; for example, giving the "sad face" she saw in Card 2 a "playful expression." Often contained in her comic perceptions were indications of self-damage, as in her humorous comment that the bat she saw in Card 1 "had better get its holes repaired." Perceptions such as the "thalidomide children" she saw in Card 7 reflected a sense of self-damage without any attempt at comic relief. In addition, a sense of a split between her head and her body was contained in her perception on Card 6 of "a goblin character with a tiny head—a comic figure with a small head and enormous feet. It thinks with its feet rather than its head."

Ellen's urge to perceive something pleasant in areas where she experienced anxiety was frequently apparent. This was clearly illustrated in Card 9, which had for her "a desert feel, perhaps a rudimentary skull with eyes." She quickly added, "It doesn't mean the end of things; there is a growing form around it; the center part is exploding in a regenerative way. There are plants coming out of the sand." Here an attempt was made to render death unthreatening and regenerative.

Identity confusion also was suggested in several of her responses, some of which was sexual in nature, as in her perception on Card 3 of two "hermaphrodites." On Card 5 she saw "an insect with antennae flying. It has a human form, trying to prove that humans can fly if they attach wings. It is going to jump off a cliff." This response appeared to reflect her efforts to reconcile seemingly unreconcilable aspects of life, tantamount to a struggle over her identity.

Summary

Both the questionnaire and the psychological tests reflected Ellen's need to minimize or deny conflicts and problems and to present her life in a favorable light. Her Rorschach responses further indicated efforts to cope with sadness with humor or playfulness. These observations were consistent with the interviewer's strong impression of her need not to look at painful aspects of her life, and appeared to support the fact that she was attracted to marijuana because it helped her to see even major problems as silly and unimportant.

Her drawings, as well as several of her Rorschach responses, suggested a split between mind and body, leading the examiner to conclude that she was capable of acting impulsively against her better judgment. This aspect of her character was evident in the interviews as well, perhaps most strikingly in the area of her relationships with men.

Both the interviews and the results of the psychological tests suggested a long history of difficulties in close personal relationships. Her sense of having been damaged as a result of the alienation she had experienced from her family, which was expressed graphically in her recurrent childhood dream of being an Indian attacking white settlers, appeared to be reflected as well in her Rorschach response of thalidomide children.

A recurrent theme in her sessions was her difficulty in establishing her identity. She seemed to feel that many of her relationships interfered with that process. She felt she had first found her own identity when away from her family at camp. She felt free to leave her husband only after her mother had died, and without the constraints of her marriage she felt life had opened up for her.

Her fears concerning death appeared to be related to the loss of herself she had often experienced in her relationships. Her Rorschach response in which she saw plants exploding in a regenerative way out of a skull and sand was seen by the examiner as reflecting a need to deal with death by making it unthreatening and turning it literally into a source of life. Her interviews similarly reflected a strong attachment to beliefs concerning reincarnation, which clearly helped her to handle her fears of death.

Her current involvement with a married man seemed to be the best relationship she had had. When last seen, she was more at peace with herself than she had previously been, and she had drastically reduced her use of marijuana. How much difficulty she would have if this man became fully available to her was not possible to predict.

Since she had stopped smoking marijuana regularly, nightmares related to her rape had returned. This was indicative of the fact that marijuana had played a role in diminishing the anxiety of what appeared to be a post-traumatic stress syndrome. It also seemed possible that her stress was being increased by the anxiety associated with the growing closeness she was experiencing in her current relationship.

MICHAEL FORENZO

Screening Session and Questionnaire

Michael Forenzo, a dark-haired, thirty-two-year-old man of medium height and build, wore a neatly trimmed beard, dark-framed glasses, and a three-piece suit, which he described as "the remains of my wardrobe" from jobs he had previously held as a TV journalist and with a major news agency. For the last two years he had been doing freelance screenwriting and aspired to become a film director.

He recently had had two brief work assignments directing off-Broadway productions but otherwise spent his time writing at home. He was married to a woman who supported him by working as a secretary for a film distributor, and they had a five-year-old daughter who attended a full-day kindergarten.

Michael had grown up in New York City and began smoking marijuana during his senior year in high school. He became a daily user toward the end of the time he was in college. For the last 11 years he had smoked four to six marijuana cigarettes a day and explained that his goal was to stay high all the time. He indicated that he smoked somewhat less on weekends when his wife and child were around, but during the week when they went off to work and school he smoked from early morning until late into the evening. He saw marijuana as helping him to feel better about almost every aspect of his life and to enjoy what he was doing to a greater extent.

On the questionnaire he indicated that the primary reason he smoked marijuana was "to get into a good disposition for work." Other reasons included to relax and relieve tension, to overcome depression, and to enhance sexual interest or pleasure. He noted, however, that on a long-term basis he felt his heavy smoking had impaired his memory and his ability to think clearly and was a major obstacle in his relationship with his parents.

He indicated that the major area of dissatisfaction in his current life was in the area of money and the standard of living he was able to afford. He also said he was unhappy with his ability to satisfy his current needs and the fact that he did not have more of a chance to do what he really wanted to do. On a scale of 1 to 10 he rated the previous year, the first since leaving his full-time job, as a 1 ("Very bad, could hardly be worse"). The present year he saw as a 6 and projected that next year would be a 9.

Recently, he had been troubled by "feeling blue" quite a bit and also feeling "tense and keyed up." He indicated that earlier in the year he had felt close to having a nervous breakdown but did not feel that way now.

Interviews

In his first session Michael talked about his work with intensity, in circumstantial detail, and with considerable grandiosity. At the same time he spoke of himself from a distance as though he was describing someone else.

He was waiting to hear about his application to a school for film directors in California. In speaking of that possibility he ruminated about what it would be like to move to California, "dousing myself in the West Coast, in that L.A. mentality." He described himself as "a very East Coast person, a New Yorker from birth." Although he did not have a strong identification with his Italian-American heritage, he said he looked to "European trends and aesthetics" and noted, "My film art has been inspired by European direction." He suspected that was "not something you would expect to find in the commercially dominated area of Los Angeles."

In describing his style of work, "At thirteen I picked up a nickname, Cecil, after Cecil B. DeMille. It had nothing to do with film or the arts. Just the way I used to boss people around. Later I was a very young manager of a New York bureau of a small network. I was always in a management position. I supervised the newsroom, 10 or 15 writers, editors, couriers. I'm good at that. I have social aplomb. These are qualities that are necessary in the business that I am pursuing, the arts."

He eventually had to be asked where his family fit into his life. He said his wife and daughter were the source of his "stability," a function he had indicated in his questionnaire that marijuana also played in his life. There was an implication that both held him together. He made it clear that his family was secondary to his work but added that he did not have to make the choice between them. In this context he noted that without marijuana his dreams "go crazy; my head literally explodes." He elaborated that his dreams were chaotic, disturbing, and apt to involve violence toward his wife and daughter. When using marijuana he did not recall his dreams.

When he was questioned as to what would happen without the stabilizing influence of his family, he indicated that he would "throw himself into the sexual arena." Noting that "a very influential book in my life was *Eros and Civilization* by Herbert Marcuse," he laughingly added, "I guess somewhere in college I felt I had too much civilization and not enough eros. I'll say this jokingly and then say it with all seriousness—I'm a pursuer of eros." The picture he then gave of his sexual life was one of isolated, fragmented experiences that he felt compelled to pursue but that left him feeling frightened and depressed.

He frequently paid prostitutes to perform fellatio on him. Twice he had had intercourse with them just to see what it was like with a woman other than his wife. He was obsessed with pornographic films, particularly films in which women were shown urinating and defecating. He spent a great deal of time spying through binoculars on a blond woman who lived across the courtyard of his building and who often walked around her apartment undressed. He masturbated many times a day usually looking at pictures that highlighted a woman's buttocks.

During the period he was being interviewed he had a sexual quarrel with his wife and reacted by following the woman he spied on when she left her apartment. He did not approach her and instead went to see some pornographic films and masturbated several times while watching them. He said that sometimes after his wife went to bed he would consider whether "to go on an eating binge, masturbate, or smoke pot."

He complained that his wife and he did not have sex frequently enough; but as he told the story, he seemed more responsible than she for their failure to get together more often. In speaking of his sexual relationship with her he began by saying, "You've got to be aware that I'm a stage director and I put great value on every gesture, on every movement." He was graphic in describing what went on sexually between them, in a style that was characterized by the following account of one disappointing encounter.

"She kneels in front of me so that I have her lower body with an embracing situation, my head on her legs or something like that. And I'm thinking I'm really starting to get going, and all of a sudden she moves up for a second to clean off some lint on the bed. We both kind of separated—the fatal separation. So that I'm at this point lying on my side, and I just give it a second. I want to see what position she's going to, whether she's going back to that position. Because if she wants to get a little involved, she'll let me know, but if she's not really, you know, going to get involved, she'd, um . . . be moving toward a quickie although I didn't—I didn't think I was. I'm on my side. So she kind of comes over and puts me on my back and gets on top of me, which was not where I wanted to be. It's her favorite position. I don't mind being there much later on. In fact, I'm more than willing, but it's no place to get started. I'll stay like this and see what she has in mind. And she starts to move our bodies together more or less, and I'm kind of going slow. I'm just kind of okay. All right, that's nice. I start to get an erection again—I had an erection through the whole thing. I mean I'm starting to get the charge again. Okay, this is going good. And she sticks it in on top of me. I didn't even know she had her diaphragm in. I wasn't there. I felt like this was somebody strange. . . . I once read a passage in the book *Gravity's Rainbow*. The protagonist had this vague recollection of when he was an infant of being tested by some crazed doctor in Cambridge, ah, lathering his genitals with some kind of substance which he's still reacting to now as an adult. And while I never had a dream like that or a feeling like that, my penis in her at that moment felt like, um, I was out on the street and a stranger opened my fly and had it there. And this is not an erotic situation. Like my privacy was infringed on. So while we're in coitus I interrupt. I speak and I said, 'What is, what's going on?' There was no way I was ready to just get it over with like that. Good night. And back in to watch TV."

Michael described himself as attracted to sin, driven by sex, and depressed about his uncontrolled, chaotic sexual life. Sometimes when he watched the woman across the courtyard he had the impulse "take a swan dive out the window." He referred several times to the fact that his astrological sign of Cancer was associated with fire and water, that is, with uncontrollable internal forces.

He said he identified with the suffering of blacks and Jews, describing himself as a sort of "nigger of the world." He pictured himself as never really "playing the game" the way others did, without having fully accepted the inevitable consequences. He read the papers every morning, and the news always made him conscious of his estrangement from society. He was sympathetic to the victories of radical movements and was bitter that others had money to pursue their interests while he had to pursue a harder course without it.

In describing his family background he said that his parents had married in their early thirties, that neither of them was particularly attractive, and that he believed it had been something of an arranged marriage. He believed his father loved his mother but that she probably had never loved him in return. When his father would put arm around his mother, she would react coldly, and Michael did not believe they had ever had much of a sexual relationship.

His father, an accountant who had to travel a considerable amount in connection with his work, was frustrated in his own ambitions and in his aspirations for Michael. He had wished to become a doctor and was referred to by family and friends both laughingly and affectionately as "Doc, the accountant." Michael described him as a nervous person who moved his hands in a compulsive manner, always worried about things, and had almost no interests outside his work and his family.

Although Michael had not felt particularly close to his father, he respected him and felt he had become dependent on him as an adolescent. He knew if he forgot to send out his college applications, for example, his father would remind him. When he broke away from the family during his college days, it was with the feeling that he did not want to be dependent on his father anymore.

He saw himself as having been closer to his mother when he was a child and described her as having been affectionate with him. He perceived her, however, as "someone who discouraged people from moving out in life." When he had wanted a boat as an adolescent, she had put it off year after year, telling him he would drown. He also described her as vindictive toward those she felt offended her and saw some parallel between his mother's behavior and the way he himself treated his wife.

His interest in books and the theater, Michael said, had derived from his mother although she was not sympathetic to his working as a director. His father also had opposed his career choice initially, saying that "only fags work in that field," but recently had become more accepting and more willing to try to help him.

He saw his mother as a religious person who functioned well and got along with people but had a narrow view of life. He added that she was very anti-sexual, stating that he was sure that had she seen him touch his penis as a boy she would have hit his hand. He saw her as overly concerned with propriety, with what the neighbors would think, for example, if his hair were not combed.

He thought he had been physically attracted to his mother but described feeling some revulsion toward physical closeness with his father. In this context he wondered if his daughter was repelled by him but thought their distance was more a matter of her not being physically affectionate with anyone.

Michael had one sibling, a sister who was two years younger. He saw himself as having been favored over her in the family. As the only son, he said it was assumed he would go to a good high school and on to college, whereas her education was not considered important. He noted that she still had considerable bitterness over this. His strongest memory of his sister was a sexual one and concerned an incident that occurred when he was fourteen and she was twelve. He reached under her dress while she was asleep, and she woke up and asked what he was doing. He lived in dread that she would mention it to their parents and claimed his fear of discussing that incident with her was responsible for some of the distance that still characterized their relationship.

He was currently not close to his parents or to his sister and stated that if they were not relatives he would not see them. He did appreciate his parents' availability as baby-sitters, however.

Michael did well in school and was active in sports until his junior year in high school, when he lost interest in both his academic and athletic activities. Although he recalled that he and his parents had had some conflict over his grades, he had no real explanation for why things had started to go badly for him in school about this time. His associations led him to the fact that he had become sexually aroused during his sophomore year. He recalled that one day during his junior year, when he had already begun to do poorly in school, he decided to skip football practice. After leaving school he bought a pornographic magazine and went home and masturbated. He believed that the cessation of his athletic interests and the awakening of his sexual desires were somehow connected. He said he had been frustrated during this period because, although he was frequently around girls, he had no girlfriend.

Although he had smoked marijuana occasionally in his senior year of high school, it was not until college that he had begun to smoke regularly and heavily. He had gone out of town to college as an engineering major but did not like it, and after a year he came back to finish college in New York. He got an apartment of his own in Greenwich Village, and his heavy smoking of marijuana became a source of great conflict with his parents. A short while later he became involved with the woman he subsequently married, whom his parents considered to be a "madonna." After Michael told them that she often smoked with him, their attitude toward marijuana softened.

During this period Michael felt he had broken with his family in terms of their values and specifically in regard to Catholicism. In place of his parents, school, and religion, which previously had helped him to integrate his life, he became deeply involved with Marcia, his future wife.

He and Marcia were the same age, had lived in the same neighborhood, and had known each other since they were youngsters. They saw each other regularly for 3 years before they married at the age of twenty-two. About a year before they married they became sexually involved, and this was the first sexual relationship for either of them.

After graduating from college Michael went on to graduate school in journalism. He then worked in television broadcasting, spent several years with a news agency, and had become a manager of a section when he quit work because he felt it interfered with his ambitions for a film career.

Since leaving his job he had had several opportunities to teach on a part-time basis but had turned down these offers, regarding them as interfering with his commitment to his work. He considered his current financial hardships the price his wife had to pay for being married to him. Although he was expansive in describing his ability, he was not optimistic about achieving success. At the same time, he indicated that he intended to continue indefinitely in his present course, whether or not he was ever successful.

Michael worked on his writing each day until midafternoon and then spent his time cleaning up the house, shopping, picking up his daughter at kindergarten, and preparing dinner. He felt that even though he did not bring in money he worked hard all day and sometimes was resentful about the restrictions his family responsibilities imposed on him.

He described his daughter as very bright, the best in her class at school, and noted that her teachers spoke of her as a caring, compassionate person. She was also artistic, talented in music, and Michael felt she had his sensitivity and ability to communicate. At home, however, he said she was often abrasive, and they got into frequent fights over her disobedience.

Michael's wife, Marcia, worked as an executive secretary for a film company. He felt that he had been responsible for stimulating her interest in film. She was being advanced rapidly in her job, and he had the fantasy that she would one day control the company and employ him as a director.

Michael related his heavy marijuana smoking most directly to his current work situation. He typically began smoking in the morning, feeling it necessary to handle the tension of facing a day of writing. He would continue to smoke throughout the day, tapering off toward the late afternoon only if he was going out to run, which he did several times a week. When his wife came home, they would smoke together to unwind, pehaps having a drink while doing so. They frequently smoked in the presence of their daughter, and around her they jokingly referred to marijuana as "the herb." Most evenings they would smoke again while watching television, and he often would continue after Marcia had gone to bed. On nights when they retired together and had sex they sometimes used Quaaludes in addition to marijuana, which he said enabled their lovemaking to last longer and "to take our sex life into new dimensions."

During the time he was being interviewed he was turned down in his application for training as a director at the film institute in California. He was deeply upset by this news and said he was tempted to fly out and try to talk his way in. In discussing this he recalled an incident in high school in which a coach took him out of an important baseball game after he had made some bad plays. Out of his anger with the coach he made remarks to encourage the other team, and the shame he had felt over his behavior had stayed with him for months.

He related the story by way of indicating that he realized his behavior had been destructive both to the team and to his relationships with his friends and said he wished to avoid behaving that way now. His linkage of the two disappointments was further illuminated when he stated that the game had been played on a May 14 and the letter from the film institute also had come on May 14. He added that when it arrived on that date, which he regarded as the worst day of the year for him, he had known it would contain bad news. Such magical thinking was characteristic of him.

When Michael was seen twice two years later, he said that everything in his life was more or less the same. In the first interview he said he was somewhat encouraged by his progress at work. He had finished writing the script for a film and said that a successful actress had indicated an interest in playing the lead. Encouraged by others who had read the script and seemed to like it, he was currently trying to raise $100,000 in order to be able to produce and direct the film. By the second interview he had become discouraged after learning that his prospects for financing the project were not working out.

Michael said that during the two years he had been working on the script, he had been buried in the house. He compared himself to Saul Bellow, who buried himself for two years while he worked on a novel. At another point he referred to another well-known novelist, who he said had seen and liked his script, adding that this writer had not become a success until he was thirty-eight.

Michael had worked as an assistant film director the past summer, a job he had gotten through his wife, who had become the distribution manager for her company and was earning $30,000 a year. He wondered whether he should take more of this kind of work, saying he thought it was good for him to get out of the house. In this context he wondered whether marijuana was helping him to avoid facing the conflict over whether or not to do so.

He said that although he was generally satisfied with his family life, he sometimes still felt imprisoned by marriage and continued to be frustrated by not having sex more often with his wife. He was still going to peep shows and saw prostitutes occasionally. He had also become involved in a brief affair with a young woman who had worked on the film with him the previous summer. He described her as a fragile person who had been hospitalized several times and had made several suicide attempts. Although he did not think it was good for them to continue to be sexually involved, he said he had remained her friend and had tried to be a comfort to her. His wife knew about his relationship with this woman although he had not told her that the relationship had been sexual.

He went on to say that he had not had any sex for ten days and did not know the reason for this. Despite his sexual frustration he had not approached his wife. He was not sure whether or not it would make him feel better if he did. He said that someone on the street had caught his eye, and he immediately thought, "Oh hell, I don't want to be bothered being attracted to an attractive girl." He added that recently a female acquaintance had kissed him and that he had subsequently dreamed about her in a sexual way.

He said that his wife was soon to leave for California in connection with her work and that he and his daughter were going to go with her in order to spend some free time together. He was not enthusiastic about the trip, however, because he felt he was "tagging along with his wife."

He then related that he had just learned that his father, who had retired to Florida, had developed lung cancer and was returning to New York the next day to seek medical care. Saying he had to be a dutiful son, he enumerated the schedule of appointments he would have to give up in order to drive his father to the doctor. When the lack of compassion he revealed for his father was commented on, Michael agreed, connecting it with traits he disliked in his father but also recognized in himself and that he described as involving a fear of people. In elaborating this he related how much he disliked his father's nervous way of always asking, "What's wrong?" when Michael would telephone him.

Michael had continued to smoke marijuana as heavily as before, and his pattern of smoking had not changed. He had begun using cocaine as well over the past year and said that although it gave him a sense of euphoria for about 20 minutes, it could not lift his depressed mood of recent months.

There was a subdued, sad quality to him during the follow-up interviews. At the end of the last session when he asked, "Is that all?" it was clear that he was seeking a connection that would guide and sustain him through the difficulties he was facing.

Psychological Tests

During the psychological testing Michael was talkative and intense, bent on impressing the examiner with his creative interests, intellectual pursuits, and unique abilities. He was often repetitive and irrelevant and conversed without maintaining normal distance and balance. He seemed to feel that everything he was saying was fresh, exciting, and bright. At the same time his concern with obtaining the results of his intelligence test appeared to reflect his need for validation of his self-view.

Michael's Full Scale IQ, as measured by the WAIS-R, was found to be 127, placing him in the superior range of functioning. He achieved a Verbal IQ of 129 and a Performance IQ of 114, with subtest scores as follows:

Verbal IQ = 129 (Superior)		*Performance IQ = 114 (High Average)*	
Information	16	Picture Completion	14
Digit Span	16	Picture Arrangement	11
Vocabulary	16	Block Design	14
Arithmetic	14	Object Assembly	11
Comprehension	12	Digit Symbol	10
Similarities	13		

Basic learned information was well retained as was his attention. However, he appeared to use intellectualization to make up for deficiencies for his understanding of people and social situations, an area that was judged to be weak in view of his relatively low score on the comprehensive subtest. Judgment was relatively underutilized and appeared to present problems in his daily living. When asked what to do if one saw smoke and fire in a movie theater, for example, he replied: "I'd get the people closest to the exit out first." This response indicated lack of insight into the nature of the problem.

On the Performance subsection he did best in Picture Completion and Block Design, tasks calling for visual concentration and alertness to detail but not requiring judgment. His Block Design scores showed excellent visual–motor coordination and a high level of efficiency in this structured task. His scores in Picture Arrangement, Object Assembly, and Digit Symbol, although noticeably lower, were all within the average range.

The 15-point discrepancy between Michael's Verbal and Performance scores, thought to reflect a lowered capacity due to emotional factors, was found to be significant at the .01 level (Naglieri, 1982). He clearly had retained skills and knowledge acquired in the past but was not currently functioning at optimal level.

The MMPI report provided the following outline of Michael's personality: "This subject apparently has an intense need to appear in a good light. In an effort to prove his social conformity, he denies the minimal kind of shortcomings that most people have and readily admit to. This suggests that he is a relatively naive person who, because of his insecurity, lacks insight into his own behavior and denies unfavorable traits both to himself and to others. He appears to be an angry, suspicious person who has difficulty with impulse control. He is evasive and defensive about acknowledging psychological problems. He tends to handle anxieties and conflicts by refusing to recognize their presence, and he utilizes rationalization as a defense mechanism. He resents authority and is likely to be argumentative and irritable in social relations, especially with the opposite sex. Although he may appear sociopathic, the possiblity of a psychotic or prepsychotic condition should be considered. Some depression, discouragement, and worry are present. He may express feelings of self-dissatisfaction and reduced initiative. He lacks confidence and has difficulty making decisions."

On the Draw-A-Person test, Michael produced two drawings (Figures 9 and 10) in which the lines were lightly filled in, faint in some places, and absent in others, indicative of a person

Figure 9.

who did not experience himself with sharp enough definition. The outer space flowed into the drawings, with the ground and the figure becoming merged, suggesting that Michael's ego boundaries were not well developed.

The male figure's facial expression was timid, hesitant, and fearful and, together with the shoulders that faded away, indicated diminished assertiveness. Saying that creating a story would be "child's play" for a professional writer, Michael gave a description of the male that contrasted considerably with his appearance: "He's a man of twenty-eight who is a concert pianist. He has committed murder. There is a certain disturbance in his eyes. His chubby face makes him look like a piano player. He's traditional-looking, but he doesn't fit in somehow. This aberration has caused his disturbance. He killed a woman—part of his difference is some kind of sexual maladjustment. He has a tough time getting along with girls. His life will not come to ruin, cer-

Figure 10.

tainly. Not suicide, but self-destruct. It's tough to see him as a good artist. He probably could sit down and dazzle us, but the music would get crazy after awhile." When asked whether this man resembled anyone he knew, he indicated that "he's similar to myself."

Michael's female figure was thought to project both his own terror and his sense of women as terrorizing him. The story he told about her, however, reflected a sensitive, artistic view of womanhood and perhaps a need for maternal care: "She looks like a figure in a painting, an idealized woman. She lives in the 1890s and is an artist's model in her thirties. It is significant she's a little older than me. She's thirty-seven. It attracts me, older people. She's a person with strong, spiritual presence. In another epic she would be the artist. There's no future in the men she's been seeing. She's never going to be happy. She sees something—the role society had made for her."

Michael said that he would like to meet her and that she barely resembled his wife. "There's a certain glow to her," he said, "which reflects a person." He went on to explain that in drawing the figure he had tried to use only one line to express head and breast in the style of Picasso, a comment that suggested the grandiosity of his self-evaluation.

Computer analysis of the 41 responses that Michael provided to the Rorschach cards revealed a number of aspects to be highly significant (see Appendix for details). First, a significantly high level of anxiety and tension was indicated through his frequent use of the achromatic portions of the blot, as well as through his overuse of shading. Shading within his form perceptions likewise indicated an excessive need for affection. In addition, his several pure-color responses pointed to a pathological lack of emotional control and possibly schizophrenia.

Michael's responses, while prolific, reflected a generally poor form quality (60%). That much of his anxiety was centered in the sexual area was indicated by responses such as that to Card 2 in which he first saw "a vagina with an open center, with a narrowing clitoris; blood surrounds the vagina. At the bottom is an expulsion of blood." This overtly sexual response indicated a lack of normal repression and extreme tensions concerning sexuality. His pure-color response of "blood" provided an example of his loss of integrated thinking processes during emotionally provocative situations. Additional sexual responses were found throughout his protocol: "breasts going out" on Card 1; "two testes and a scrotum" on Card 6; and "a vagina and an anus" on Card 7.

Michael's sense of estrangement was reflected in several percepts of "aliens" or "alien creatures." His overall emotional fragility seemed to be expressed in his response to Card 9, which he saw as "an exploding brain."

Summary

Michael's responses to the questionnaire, although revealing some problems with his self-esteem, did not directly reflect the degree of disturbance in his personal life that was suggested through the interviews and psychological tests. Although he labeled his life over the past year as very bad, his present life as somewhat good, and his expectations for his future life as very good, the interviews revealed far more torment and despair over his current situation and his future expectations. His questionnaire responses appeared to reflect his attempts to avoid dealing with present difficulties by telling himself he had already surmounted them or certainly would do so in the near future.

His questionnaire responses on the role of marijuana in his life indirectly suggested his difficulties by the sheer number of ways in which he saw marijuana as improving his life. As short-term benefits of marijuana he included an increased ability to forget his troubles and problems, to relax and enjoy life, and to have a good time with friends; an increased enjoyment of food and sex; increased ability to avoid boredom and feelings of frustration, anger, and depression; increased excitement and enthusiasm for life; improved relations with spouse; and decreased physical discomfort. Under long-term benefits of marijuana he included an enhanced ability to cope with and solve life's problems, to overcome worry and anxiety, and to enjoy life; an increase in self-understanding, understanding of other people, and creativity; and an increase in his level of excitement and enthusiasm for life, his overall happiness, and his general satisfaction with life.

No other subject participating in the study indicated so large a number of benefits that were derived from smoking marijuana. Michael's interviews suggested that his questionnaire responses, rather than being an exaggeration, reflected the number of ways in which he felt unable to deal with life with his own resources.

The mixture of alienation and aggression evident in his clinical interviews was reflected in his responses to the drawings he provided as part of the psychological tests. He identified directly with the the man he drew and described him as a concert pianist with a potential for madness, a misfit, and a murderer. Grandiosity was reflected as well in his description of his female figure, which he said had been drawn with the breast and face in one line "in the style of Picasso." Although direct evidence of grandiosity was not found in the content of his Rorschach responses, the high number of responses (41) in itself pointed in this direction.

Michael's Rorschach protocol reflected a lack of emotional control and a significantly high level of anxiety and tension, aspects of his personality that were evident as well throughout his clinical interviews. The psychological report's emphasis on his excessive needs for affection also was consistent with the child-like dependency seen clinically.

Although clinically the absence of delusions, hallucinations, or incoherence did not warrant a diagnosis of schizophrenia on a basis of current diagnostic criteria (*Diagnostic and Statistical Manual of Mental Disorders*, 1980), Michael had clearly deteriorated from a previous level of functioning. The chaotic, fragmented, obsessed quality of his sexual life, his magical thinking and grandiosity, and his eccentric behavior were indicative of a schizotypal personality.

In the interviews he described marijuana as one of the stabilizing forces in his life, helping him during the day to ease the tension of working and of dealing with "the blank page." In the evening he used it as a break with the working day, and its use before going to bed helped to prevent chaotic disturbing dreams that were apt to involve violence toward his wife and daughter. By reducing his overall anxiety, marijuana did indeed seem to help him hold himself together. At the same time it appeared to foster the unrealistic, grandiose, uncompromising approach he had to his career and his family.

IRENE ROUSSEAU

Screening Session and Questionnaire

Irene Rousseau was a tall, somewhat overweight woman of thirty-two with a fair complexion and straight blond hair. She had been married for ten years, had no children, and was employed as an administrative assistant in a large corporation. She also was attending a local college one evening a week in order to complete an undergraduate degree in biology, with the goal of eventually working in the field of genetics.

Irene had been born in the Midwest but spent most of her life in the New York metropolitan area. She had begun smoking marijuana at the age of fifteen and became a regular heavy user about four years later. Currently she smoked about three marijuana cigarettes a day, primarily in the evening on workdays but throughout the day when she was not working. On the questionnaire she listed a wide variety of reasons as motivating her marijuana use, including to relax and relieve tension, to deepen her self-understanding, to get away from her problems and troubles, and to overcome depression. She also indicated that she smoked marijuana in order to enhance her pleasure when reading, which she described as her favorite leisure time activity.

She saw marijuana as improving her life in almost every respect in the short term and identified nothing as usually made worse for her while high. On a long-term basis, however, she indicated that marijuana impaired her general level of energy, her ambition, and her educational progress and achievement.

On the questionnaire Irene described herself as "pleased" or "delighted" with most aspects of her life, particularly with her relationships with other people. She felt "terrible," however, about the amount of money she had, the amount of pay she got for the amount of work she did, the physical conditions in her job, and how consistent and understandable her world seemed to be. Overall, she rated her life as a 6 on a scale of 1 to 10, down from last year, which she rated as having been an 8. Next year, she felt, would be a 7.

She indicated that recently she had felt extremely bothered by "feeling blue," and her responses to some items suggested some problems with self-esteem ("At times I think I am no good at all;" "I certainly feel useless at times"). Some time ago, she said, she had been close to having a nervous breakdown but felt she was completely over it now.

Interviews

Irene was open and unguarded, relating the many traumas of her life in a relaxed and good-natured manner, often using humor to make her point. At the same time she seemed removed from her feelings about the painful events she recounted.

As she told the story of her use of marijuana and other drugs, it was interwoven with the illness and death of her parents during the period when she was between the ages of sixteen and twenty-two. While Irene was in high school her mother contracted tuberculosis and was confined to bed and in hospitals much of the time. Her father developed a rapidly fatal cancer during her first year of college, and because she was their only child, she dropped out of school to help with the care of both parents. A close friends of hers had died of cancer during her last year of high school, and she had felt emotionally torn apart by that experience. She resolved not to let this happen with her father's impending death and said she refused to let herself think about it. She started smoking marijuana heavily and also used heroin for several months during the last stage of his illness. She stopped using heroin soon after he died.

Irene saw her mother as having "gone to pieces" after her father's death, saying, "She didn't really want to live anymore. She didn't care about anything. She would not go out, and she just kind of sat around and moped." She described her mother as having broken off relations with her father's family because she did not want to be reminded of her loss. Several years later she refused to come to Irene's wedding, claiming she did not want to see her in-laws.

Following the death of her father, her mother's attitude toward Irene became antagonistic, although at the same time she wanted her to be available to care for her. They fought constantly, and Irene left New York for California "to get away from my mother, be a hippie, and live in Haight-Ashbury." While there she worked as a secretary, "hung around," and used a great deal of LSD.

She came home when her mother's health became worse, but shortly thereafter her mother moved to the Midwest to live with her sister. Irene stayed in New York, where she became involved with a man named George who was then a college student; they married two years later. Several months after their marriage she and her husband, who had no prior history of use, began using heroin in conjunction with their relationship with a male friend who lived with them.

Shortly before her mother died Irene went out to visit her and felt devastated by the fact that her aunt blamed her mother's deterioration and impending death on Irene's neglect. Although she knew that in some way her mother wanted to die, refusing to see a doctor in the last year of her illness, Irene felt she had been selfish by leaving home while her mother was sick and later by not being willing to move with her to her aunt's house. She described herself as having felt worthless in the face of her aunt's accusations.

During the period after her mother's death Irene and George became involved with amphetamines in addition to the heroin to which they eventually became addicted for several years. At the peak of their habit they needed $90 a day; George dropped out of school, and they sold drugs in order to manage. With her husband's acceptance she sometimes slept with other men for money, which they used to purchase heroin. Both she and George enrolled in several different methadone programs; however, none of them seemed to work. He became physically abusive to her, and they separated for a period of several years.

Irene said she was unable to tolerate living alone and described several destructive relationships with men, all of whom were also drug users or heavy drinkers. In talking about this period of her life she said, "The problem was all those years I had all that trouble, I felt so terrible about myself. I'd look in the mirror and say what a terrible, disgusting person you are, and there is no reason for you to be here. You've never done anything good for anybody in your whole life." She became deeply depressed, cut her wrists, and took an overdose of drugs in a serious suicide attempt. After being comatose in a hospital for several days, she was transferred to a psychiatric unit for treatment for several months. She and George eventually got back together with the understanding they would stop using heroin, and for the past five years they had been successful in doing so.

About this time one of Irene's friends developed rapidly degenerative multiple schlerosis. Irene spent a year helping to care for this young woman and was with her when she died. She subsequently helped the woman's mother, who also had to deal with the death of her husband four months later. As Irene described it, "I felt pretty good that I had done something for somebody, so then I was able to start feeling better about myself."

Her husband made radio commercials for a large charitable

organization, and Irene was capable and successful in her administrative capacity. They were both dissatisfied with their salaries, however, and could barely manage their house and car payments. Although Irene took courses in college and aspired to become a genetics counsellor or to work in a drug rehabilitation program, she put off doing anything about her work situation. Despite the fact that she was not being adequately compensated for her current work, she said she had many close friends there and would be reluctant to leave them.

She claimed she loved her husband, although she described him as selfish and unsociable. She said he often would eat everything in the refrigerator without thinking to save anything for her. He did not stop her from seeing friends but would not join her in social activities. She also felt he was resentful that she earned more than he did.

Although she expressed dissatisfaction over the lack of pleasurable involvement she had with George and with his lack of consideration of her needs, she was out of touch with her real anger toward him. Her feelings, however, were quite evident in her dreams. After a day in which he had refused to go swimming with her and had stayed home and eaten all the food she had prepared for both of them, he wanted her to give him a new deodorant she had bought for herself, despite the fact that she had purchased one for him that he had asked her to buy. She refused and dreamed that night that he asked for his deodorant and she told him it was in the toilet. Her dream graphically expressed what she felt he deserved from her for not being more giving. Prior to talking about the dream she had not been in touch with her irritation with him, perhaps because she feared she would "go to pieces" if something were to happen to him or to their relationship.

Irene had smoked marijuana on a daily basis since the time her father had become sick, even during the period she was heavily involved with other drugs. In her current pattern she smoked in the car on the way to work, sometimes during the day, while returning from work, and sometimes with her husband in the evening, but she enjoyed it most at night while reading science fiction in the bathtub. She related her use of marijuana to a lack of excitement in her marriage and in her life and felt her use of it relieved boredom. Although she stressed the beneficial effects of marijuana, she indicated she might do more to improve her life if she did not smoke so heavily.

Irene said that she thought a lot about raising a child but did not want to have one of her own because she did not want all the bother of infancy. She also felt she could not afford to stop working. During the years when she had been heavily involved with drugs she had twice become pregnant. She explained that she had had an abortion in both instances because she and her husband were afraid of the possible consequences to the child of the drugs she was taking.

In this context Irene indicated that since she herself had been adopted at the age of six months, she would like to adopt a child in order to give someone else what had been given to her. She described her adoption as having posed no problem to her. She said that when she was three her parents had read her a story about a "chosen child" and that except for one nun at Catholic school no one ever humiliated her about it.

She recalled that when she was twelve she opened a box belonging to her father and discovered her natural mother's name and that she was Irish. She made some attempts to find her mother but was told the records had been destroyed. In speaking of her desire to locate her natural mother, Irene said that she was interested in finding out about any genetic illnesses in her family in order to know what to expect in her own life. In response to questioning, however, she indicated that she did not connect her academic interest in genetics with having been adopted. Another reason she gave for wanting to find her natural mother was to learn the time of her birth because of her interest in astrology; she added that people born under her sign (Libra) have trouble with decisions and keep their anger inside.

Besides her adoption, the aspect of her childhood that Irene most emphasized was the fact that her father's job as an accountant for a large corporation required the family to move every six months between Milwaukee and Chicago. When she was eight they moved to Connecticut and finally to a suburb of New York City. In discussing these moves her focus was on the instability and insecurity that had resulted from frequently changing schools and the need to make new friends.

Although she tried at first to present her family as having had no problems until her parents became ill, Irene's childhood recollections suggested a somewhat different picture. Except for one vacation and one time when her parents took her to an amusement park, Irene did not recall her family's having done anything together. Her parents were not physically affectionate with her or with each other. At least as far back as when she was twelve, Irene remembered them as having slept separately. Neither of them had any outside interests; her father spent almost all his free time working around the house, and her mother would read.

After moving to the New York area her mother got a job as a saleswoman in the garment industry, and what time she and Irene spent together took place when they went shopping. Although she reassured herself that her mother must have liked to have taken her along on those shopping trips, Irene said they were never close, never played together, and that her mother did not seem to enjoy being with her. She added that her mother was a stubborn person who never changed her mind, had to have things her way, and never permitted Irene to express her feelings.

Irene's earliest memories involved painful or unpleasant events associated with her mother: at three, drinking the phenobarbital her mother used for migraine headaches and being forced to vomit; also at three, putting a bead up her nose and crying hysterically while her mother rushed her to a doctor; at four, being angry with her mother and grinding her crayons into the floor with her rocking chair.

Her early memories of her father, however, were pleasant. He sometimes read stories to her and occasionally took her with him when he went to pitch horseshoes. She had felt close to him and respected him as a bright, likable, caring person.

She recalled two recurrent dreams from her childhood. In one an alligator was devouring the city of Milwaukee, suggesting a frustrated emotional hunger going back to her earlier years. When this possibility was suggested to her, she said it would not surprise her because she was always an insecure person. In the other dream she was with her mother and was afraid of an eagle that might swoop down and snatch her away. This appeared to indicate a fear of being separated from her adopted parents as she had been from her natural mother. In discussing this she vaguely recalled her mother having threatened to "give me back" when she was young and that her father had once made such a threat when she was an adolescent.

Her parents sent her to Catholic school, which she hated because of the regimentation. When she was in 10th grade she made a gesture of running away from home, and her parents transferred her to a public school. Irene perceived open difficulties with her mother as dating to the time she was a teenager. Their frequent disagreements centered on Irene's staying out late, drinking, and riding in cars or on motorbikes with boys. By this time her mother was sick with tuberculosis and in bed much of the time, and Irene tried to avoid arguments with her while doing what she pleased.

Her father had not become involved in the difficulties Irene experienced with her mother. A close friend who was an astrologer had the theory that he might have been her natural father. Irene felt this might have explained both her mother's distance from her and her father's warmth and closeness. She seemed to like this possibility, although it caused her some anxiety in that her father's family tended to lose their hearing in their fifties.

Her paternal relatives were emotionally important to her and were involved with her, although they had known her primarily as a young child. Her grandmother had left Irene some money when she died several years ago. In relating this she said, "I couldn't believe it. I felt so loved, I was just the happiest. It was such a good therapy for me to go out there. And I remember at my grandmother's funeral I started crying afterward, and they all came over and they put their arms around me, and I couldn't stop crying because it was like all the crying I had wanted to do. I had never had anyone who would make me feel better just by putting their arms around me since my father had died."

In talking about death Irene expressed her belief that everyone comes from a pool of energy and returns to that state after death. She said her astrologer friend believed in reincarnation, and although she said she did not, she was open to being persuaded. Her friend had suggested that Irene was actually an old person and new only to this planet. Irene thought that might explain why she had always felt alien and out of place.

Her sense of being alien seemed to be related to her passion for science fiction. She believed there were other beings "out there" in the universe and said if they ever came for her she would be ready to go. She appeared to be hopeful of such a possibility, and when this was pointed out, she said it would be the "adventure of a lifetime."

When Irene was seen for a follow-up two years later, she had a new position in her company as a computer programmer and described her life as better in some ways and worse in others. It was better because she liked her new job much more. She and George also had bought a beautiful house, and they were getting along better and doing more things together. He was now willing to socialize with her and had started going with her to parties and even to the beach. Her life was worse mainly because "we sold our soul to get the house" and were financially very pressured as a consequence. Her entire salary was going to pay for the mortgage.

Although she liked her work, she was dissatisfied that she had received neither the title nor the salary that should have gone with the position. She had filed a sex-discrimination complaint against her firm. Her immediate boss was supporting her claim, but a vice-president at the firm who saw her as too outspoken was blocking her. She related a recent dream in which that man was trying to kill her and someone killed him instead.

Irene said that she had learned to be more self-reliant and to deal with her husband better. Instead of getting angry she decided he was not going to change, that "he is the way he is" and that she would accept it. She might have liked him to visit his grandmother, who was dying, or to have visited his mother in the hospital when she was there to undergo a hysterectomy for cancer. But she said she knew he would not do that sort of thing, and rather than saying anything about it she had kept quiet; as a consequence she thought they got along better.

She complained that he had been traveling a lot in connection with his work and never called her or even told her exactly where he was going. Once when she had needed to reach him, she had to get his location from his firm. All of that, she felt, was part of his overall lack of consideration. When asked, she said she did not worry about whether he was with another woman, adding that although she did not think he was, what she did not know did not hurt her. She said that was her philosophy toward life for the most part.

She felt George had improved a little, however. Now, when he thought about it, he would occasionally be a little considerate, if only because he realized it would result in her treating him better. She also felt she was more self-reliant now and said that although she would miss him if they were not together, she would be able to manage without him if she had to. She added that she had learned not to depend on him as a way of protecting herself because "he could die, get killed on the parkway or something."

In recent years she had become quite close to her husband's parents and grandmother and continued to be close to several of her father's relatives. She had recently been visited by her uncle and said she had cried when he left, at least in part because he reminded her so much of her father. She spoke with her uncle about genealogy, a topic in which he was also interested, and he promised to help her find out more about her natural mother.

Irene still smoked marijuana every day, although she thought she might have cut down a little on the amount, partially because marijuana was currently hard to obtain. She drank a little more as a consequence, particularly after work, saying that if she did not have marijuana she was apt to have a martini. She also thought she might be smoking a little less because she spent less time in the car now that she lived closer to work. She and her husband still smoked together every evening, and she still loved smoking in the bathtub while reading science fiction. She said she expected to smoke the rest of her life unless she became persuaded it was bad for her.

Psychological Tests

Irene maintained a relaxed, good-natured, and occasionally humorous manner throughout the testing session. At times she came across as girlish and naive but overall demonstrated a strong sense of down-to-earth realism.

The WAIS-R was administered, in which she scored a Full Scale IQ of 124, with a Verbal IQ of 129 and a Performance IQ of 110. These results place Irene in the superior range of functioning. The 19-point discrepancy between Irene's Verbal and Performance scores was found to be highly significant (Naglieri, 1982) and suggested difficulties in converting ideas into action. On the 11 subscales of the test she scored as follows:

Verbal IQ = 129 (Superior)		Performance IQ = 110 (Bright Normal)	
Information	14	Picture Completion	14
Digit Span	12	Picture Arrangement	11
Vocabulary	16	Block Design	12
Arithmetic	14	Object Assembly	9
Comprehension	16	Digit Symbol	11
Similarities	15		

Irene showed well-developed and well-utilized abilities in concept formation and reasoning. However, her attention and the ability to maintain a fixed, relevant focus appeared to be interfered with by moderate anxiety, resulting in deficits in functioning in the Digit Span and various of the Performance subtests.

The MMPI report provided the following outline of Irene's personality: "The unwillingness of this subject to admit the relatively minor faults that most people have suggests that she is a person with strong needs to be seen by others, and perhaps by herself, as an unusually virtuous person. She has low scores on the clinical scales, which usually suggests an absence of serious psychopathology. She appears to be an energetic person whose impulsiveness may cause difficulties in interpersonal relations. She is likely to be sociable, open, and friendly but also may be somewhat self-centered and immature."

On the Draw-A-Person Test, Irene first drew a picture of a man (Figure 11) whose general appearance and "spacy" facial expression reflected reduced self-respect and lowered self-esteem. The mechanism of denial was suggested, however, in the way negative self-image was tucked away behind a pose of nonchalance. The hand drawn to the gential region, and yet

Figure 11.

with the absence of a fly, pointed to psychosexual concerns. The sparseness of the hair added to the sense of diluted masculinity, and Irene's need to depreciate or minimize men was suggested in the fact that the male figure was off-balance and smaller than the woman she later drew.

She described the male figure as follows: "This is a mellow kind of person. He's about thirty years old. He just got out of college and obtained an entry-level position at IBM and he feels set for the future. He has an older brother, a lawyer, a sister who is studying physics, and a father who is successful and earns sixty thousand a year. Right now he's at a tennis match, at Rye. This is who I should have married. Not really; I would have been financially set but bored. He's leaning against the fence watching some girls—he's not gay; that would have upset his parents. One of the girls comes over, and they have some small talk. Eventually, he'll become an alcoholic. In two years he'll marry a

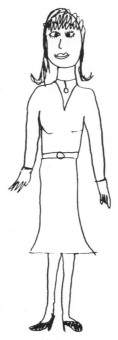

Figure 12.

nurse. He had to have his appendix out. They fall in love. He got better, and everything worked out. He has grandchildren, and lives till eighty-seven and dies in his sleep."

Her remarks suggested some dissatisfaction in regard to her husband as well as a sense of men as dependent and emotionally inadequate. A heightened sense of social class also was indicated in her story.

The female figure Irene drew (Figure 12) had crossed eyes and a facial expression almost as spacy as that of her male drawing. These qualities suggested that Irene experienced herself as somewhat ludicrous or silly and, like those of the male figure, reflected low self-esteem. The agitated lines of hair over the crossed eyes added a feeling that she experienced her thoughts (the site behind these lines being the head) as jumpy and anxious. Psychosexual concerns were again suggested by the sparseness of the breasts and the superficial effort to emphasize femininity through the necklace, the exaggerated eyelashes, and the lipstick.

Irene's description of the woman was as follows: "This is his [the male figure's] wife. No! She's really not this ugly. She is about twenty-five and single. Actually, she's divorced. She married her childhood sweetheart, but it didn't work out. She's an executive for Proctor and Gamble. She has money. She goes skiing, travels, has dinner dates, and sometimes spends the nights with them. But she's mainly career-oriented. She's looking toward the future. About ten years go by. She changes jobs to an international company, travels to Australia, and meets a rancher with a thousand acres. They get married and she quits her job; she learns to be a rancher. They'll have one baby and adopt stray babies. Her husband gets killed in a ranch accident, and she lives happily ever after and dies at ninty-two. She's eaten by a kangaroo—not really."

This story appeared to indicate a wish on Irene's part to attain fulfillment by separating from her husband. While suggesting a perception that the good things in life could only be attained through a man, it reflected a vision of life as being truly enjoyable only without one. The playful quality of the story appeared to represent a form of denial of the discontent and conflict that obviously were present.

Computer analysis of Irene's 20 responses to the Rorschach cards indicated a high intelligence with good problem-solving ability, based on her above-average number of whole responses (15). Anxiety, apprehension, and tension, reflected in her frequent use of achromatic color; and an excessive need for affection, reflected in her overuse of shading, also were found to be significant (see Appendix for details).

These concerns seemed to derive from unmet early dependency needs. Images of babies, the birth process, and eating were recurrent in her protocol. On Card 1 she saw a bird "getting ready to build a nest." On Card 3 she saw a uterus with a "fetus curled up in there." On Card 6 she saw a paramecium "sucking in some food." Despite her anxieties, she evidenced fair ties to reality with a form level of 71 percent.

Summary

Irene's responses to the marijuana questionnaire were generally consistent with the interviews in her assertions that marijuana helped her to relax, relieve tension, and get away from her problems. Both on the questionnaire and in the interviews she indicated an awareness that marijuana impaired her general level of energy, her ambition, and her educational progress and achievement.

Despite feeling unfairly treated at work, she was afraid of losing her friends if she changed jobs. Her distaste for moving and making new friends appeared to be related to the anxiety created by her family's frequent moves when she was young. The deaths of her friend, her father, and her mother in a relatively brief period undoubtedly contributed as well to her fears of separation and abandonment. Marijuana clearly encouraged her passivity and her attempts to avoid recognizing and dealing with her problems.

Both the psychological report and the interviews suggested the damaged self-esteem caused by early emotional deprivation. Both sets of data provided evidence of a basic emotional frustration in her early relationship with her mother, in particular, that appeared to have left her especially vulnerable to the subsequent loss of her parents.

She indicated on the questionnaire that smoking marijuana helped to deepen her self-understanding. Her belief in this regard, however, was not supported by the interviews. Her strong need to avoid looking at her early family relationships, because to do so would be painful, extended to not wishing to deal with her dissatisfaction with her marriage. She was somewhat more willing to acknowledge her dissatisfaction at work although there too she was reluctant to make active efforts to change the situation.

Smoking virtually every night in the bathtub while reading science fiction helped her to escape from the boredom and emotional frustration of her marriage and from the frustration and lack of recognition she experienced in her job. She avoided facing problems in her marriage because she was afraid that to do so would make her depressed and suicidal again, and she feared she might collapse if her relationship with her husband ended. At least in part this fear appeared to have been a result of seeing what had happened to her mother after her father's death.

CHAPTER 5

CONCLUSIONS

We began this study with the goal of understanding the role of marijuana in the psychosocial adaptation of adults who had used the drug heavily for a considerable number of years. Through the written questionnaire completed by a large, broad-based group of daily marijuana-smoking adults and the intensive study of cases we selected from this group, a picture of the adaptive significance of marijuana emerged. In this chapter we first identify and discuss the functions of heavy marijuana use for the adults we studied, drawing in particular on the material we obtained from the psychodynamic interviews. It is important to remember that the subjects who participated in this study were those whose use of marijuana was heavy and long-term. Care must thus be taken in generalizing the findings to a broader population of adult users.

The next section of the chapter contrasts the functions of marijuana for adults with what we had learned about the adaptive significance of the drug in our earlier study of adolescents. We then discuss and evaluate the unique data-gathering approach taken in this study, comparing and contrasting what was learned from the various methods we incorporated: the written questionnaire, the interviews, and the psychological tests. Finally, some general conclusions are drawn about the adults we studied and heavy long-term marijuana use.

THE FUNCTIONS OF MARIJUANA

Through the intensive process of the unstructured interviews we had an opportunity to obtain a picture of how daily, heavy marijuana use functioned in the context of the individual's overall psychosocial development. The use of psychodynamic interviewing techniques, including challenging and exploring defenses and eliciting dream and fantasy material, allowed us to move far beyond the person's thoughts or beliefs about marijuana to a point where use of the drug could be seen in terms of the unique dynamic functions it performed for the individual. In most cases our findings did not contradict the reasons individuals had given on the questionnaire for smoking marijuana but rather provided a context and perspective that rendered them meaningful.

Among all 15 cases the functions of heavy marijuana use were found to be related to the individual's particular life circumstances and, more important, to how he or she perceived them. Seeing the subjects over a considerable period of time (usually about two years) allowed us to observe the degree to which changes in circumstances were accompanied by alterations in both the individual's pattern of marijuana use and the particular functions the drug performed for him or her.

Although for each individual daily marijuana smoking could be seen to have multiple psychological uses, it is helpful to look at several distinct functions that appeared consistently among our cases. These are discussed below under the separate headings of self-awareness, work, and personal relationships.

Self-Awareness

Marijuana is often thought to be a drug that encourages contemplation, and most of our subjects saw it that way. Most felt it increased their understanding of themselves and others, making them more philosophical and insightful about what was going on around them.

Yet we were impressed that marijuana permitted each of the individuals we studied to lead an unexamined life strikingly free of introspection. Marijuana enabled Ellen Thornton, Irene Rousseau, Jeffrey Gordon, and Daniel Pollock to avoid looking at the pain and frustration of their early lives and to avoid seeing the effects of their early experiences on their personality and character. The use of marijuana to avoid self-awareness in adult life was strikingly exemplified by Daniel's having gone through two long-term marriages with no sense of his own contribution to their failure, by Michael Forenzo's living in a world of grandiose fantasy in which the limitations and realities of his life could be almost totally ignored, by Jeffrey Gordon's use of passive resignation to avoid awareness of his discontent with his lack of success in both work and personal relationships, by Irene Rousseau's ability to detach herself from the frustrations of her marriage, by Ellen Thornton's belief in astrology as a guide to relationships and her reluctance to look at the impact of her own needs and character on her attachments, and by Emily Leone's ability to escape from commitment through her "fantasy tickets."

How is the daily marijuana users' view of their heightened awareness to be reconciled with the absence of introspection that seems to go with the drug? The interviews indicated that becoming detached from the feelings and reality of current situations gave these individuals the impression of transcending the situation and augmenting their perspectives. Irene Rousseau told herself that her husband's selfishness and lack of consideration were not important to her. She insisted, "That's just the way he is and I refuse to let it bother me." But she needed marijuana, science fiction, and a warm bath to maintain the illusion that she was not troubled by his behavior.

On the basis of those with whom we worked, it appeared to be less insight than the transcendence of painful vision that characterizes heavy marijuana smokers. Detachment enabled these men and women to see their problems as less important; the ability to minimize was consistently confused with insight.

Mystical experience involves a comparable process. Carlos

Castaneda (1973) tells the story of a man who saw his son fall from a bridge and was at his side when he died. The father, seeing his son's death as part of the flux of life and death, shed no tears and felt no pain.

The quality of thinking evident in the Castaneda episode involves such a degree of abstraction as to make reality irrelevant. Divorcing thinking or feeling from the situation results in an impersonal vision that can be confused with what is commonly called a "philosophic" attitude. True for everyone and no one, such mystical perceptions reflect an inherent depersonalization and differ from a genuine philosophic attitude in that they do not derive from knowledge of self in relation to others and the human condition. Rather, they have as their source the desire to escape from self into abstraction. Thinking as a means of unraveling the problems of self is not furthered but rather avoided by suppressing the thoughts and feelings that are unique to oneself and that make up one's personality.

With few exceptions, the 15 subjects whom we studied seldom remembered their dreams, and many felt that smoking marijuana inhibited such recollections. Michael Forenzo was aware of disturbing nightmares involving violence to his wife and child when he did not smoke heavily before going to sleep. For Ellen Thornton the need to avoid dreams seemed related to the rape-induced traumatic nightmares that preceded her heavy marijuana smoking. Those subjects like Irene Rousseau, who dreamed with strong affect of her irritation with her husband, were out of touch with such affect in their waking life and tended to ignore their dreams. Ellen Thornton's reaction to her recollection of a recurrent childhood dream of being an Indian at war with whites was to believe that it reflected her existence in a previous life. The tendency to look for mystical rather than psychological interpretations of experience was characteristic of many of our subjects, most particularly the women.

The reluctance of the daily marijuana users to think about human situations was underlined by the avoidance of reading anything but superficial material for pleasure. Reading that stimulated introspective comparison to other people's lives was specifically avoided. So too was intellectual activity that was not directly related to one's work. This was true of the most educated among the group we studied, such as Ellen Thornton, a writer, and Daniel Pollock, a lawyer. Irene Rousseau, who did read, ready only science fiction, always in the bathtub while high on marijuana. For Irene, her reading, like her bath and her smoking, was a form of escape from her present life.

Work

For some, like Jeffrey Gordon, who always smoked on the way to and from work, marijuana fostered a resigned acceptance of a lack of occupational success. Irene Rousseau and Emily Leone, who were reasonably successful in what they did but were operating well below their abilities, saw marijuana as enabling them to avoid the challenge of their own capabilities. For others, like Michael Forenzo, heavy marijuana smoking was part of a more total withdrawal from the competitive aggression of the working world and the responsibility of providing for his wife and family. The change he made in his life at the age of twenty-six, leaving a job in which he had experienced success but also considerable demands and competition, paralleled the withdrawal behavior often seen in adolescents reacting to the pressures of school.

Others, like lawyer Daniel Pollock who had been raised to perform and achieve and who saw himself as a "cut-throat bastard" at work, would not smoke during the working day. During evenings and weekends, however, they needed massive quantities of marijuana to reduce their aggressive, driven quality and to permit them to relax and to enjoy social relationships.

For women like Ellen Thornton, who avoided marijuana during the working day, the drug was perceived as helping to put aside the responsibilities of the adult world and allowing them to "play." For others, like Emily Leone and Jeffrey Gordon, the responsibility from which they needed to escape was parenthood.

Marijuana was not merely an escape from work and responsibility in the lives of our subjects. The function of marijuana in reducing tension and anxiety sufficiently to diminish a sense of diffuseness and fragmentation was also important to some. Michael Forenzo believed marijuana enabled him to write and provided stability in an otherwise chaotic life. Another of our 15 cases, a successful writer and film director, found marijuana necessary to permit her to focus on any one of her numerous projects without being distracted by all the others.

How is it that daily use of marijuana focused attention and permitted some to work, whereas others avoided it at work, seeing it as interfering with their ambition and energy? The answer seems to be that although marijuana detaches and therefore distances focus, it also calms and permits some selective vision.

Personal Relationships

Marijuana played an important role in the personal relationships of virtually all of our subjects. For those who began heavy marijuana smoking as adolescents living with their parents, marijuana was usually significant in either open or covert rebellion against their families. In addition, it appeared to facilitate their social access into a group of friends who were also seen as opposed to parental values. For Irene Rousseau marijuana served both purposes. It was part of her protest against her mother's treatment of her and marked the beginning of relationships primarily with drug users and abusers.

When adult relationships were frustrating and painful, marijuana reduced anxiety, anger, and depression for these individuals. In facilitating their detachment from the unpleasant reality of a current situation, it enabled many of the subjects to exist for years in troubled relationships without feeling any urgency to do anything about them. Such detachment diminished the reality of the other person, permitting individuals like Emily Leone and Daniel Pollock to be able, by being high during sexual relationships, to achieve satisfaction with marital partners whom they otherwise found distasteful.

Marijuana made involvement possible for some, creating an illusion of intimacy while restricting closeness and commitment. This was true for subjects who were involved in relationships where there was no evident conflict or unhappiness but where closeness and deep connection were evidently feared. Irene Rousseau, Daniel Pollock, and Jeffrey Gordon were good examples. Although Emily Leone's perception of commitment as akin to entrapment, suffocation, and death provided a particularly graphic expression of the fear of closeness, this theme also was echoed in others of our selected cases.

The need to restrict closeness was paradoxically linked to the perception of many of the subjects that marijuana enhanced their sexual pleasure. That enhancement for the most part involved sexual fantasies or behavior in which someone was included other than or in addition to the man or woman with whom they were most involved. Dan was aroused by behavior or fantasies that marijuana stimulated in which he was having sex with one woman and was being watched by another. Emily's fantasies involved her and her husband having sex with other partners with each other's knowledge or having sex together with another couple. Her husband's recent affair was welcomed by her, giving her greater freedom to do the same. They saw their relationship as strong enough to survive infidelity. It seemed more likely that it could not have survived without it.

The use of marijuana to keep emotional distance was nowhere more evident than in the relationships between the heavy marijuana users and their children. Emily Leone was typical of mothers we saw who smoked while caring for their children, maintaining that rather than being an obstacle to a relationship, being high on marijuana relaxed them enough to enjoy being with their children. The strong objections their children had to their smoking suggested that the youngsters perceived that something quite different was going on. Also revealing was Emily's attitude that if she had a chance to live her life over she would not have children. Like Emily, the other subjects who were mothers were conscientious and concerned but saw their relationships with their children as a heavy burden that smoking helped to lighten. Those fathers who were directly involved in caring for their children had similar attitudes. Michael Forenzo's frequent dreams of violence to his daughter, whom he cared for with some reluctance while his wife worked, were not surprising. On the other hand, Daniel Pollock, who did not smoke when with his children, treated them much as he did his employees, criticizing their performance in ways that inevitably alienated them from him.

Comparison of Adult and Adolescent Marijuana Users

We came to this study after some years of work with high school and college youngsters who were heavy marijuana smokers. The comparison of the role of marijuana in the lives of the younger and older subjects provides a perspective on the use of the drug in psychosocial adaptation.

In our work with adolescents who were heavy marijuana users, we saw the drug used to defy parents, to control rage, to express self-destructive wishes, to help in withdrawing from conflicts over achievement and ambition, and to support fantasies of grandiosity and effortless success. These same factors were often present in our adult cases but were manifested in quite different ways.

The defiance of parents that was reflected in the use of marijuana and in other behaviors of adolescent marijuana users had generally evolved in the adult users into a more general break with parental and conventional societal values. It was evident in the emancipation felt by Ellen Thornton who broke away from life as a doctor's wife in favor of what she viewed as a more unrestricted lifestyle. It was most evident in those like Michael Forenzo, who identified himself with revolutionary groups and minority causes and referred to himself as a "nigger of the world." For most of the regular marijuana users, their efforts to obtain a constant supply of the drug, to sell marijuana if only to pay for their own use, and to use the drug while avoiding difficulties with the law were associated with a view they held of themselves, often with some satisfaction, as behaving in ways that did not have societal sanction.

Among the adolescents, marijuana was often used in a grossly self-destructive way that alienated parents and siblings and led to school failures and to encounters with police. With such youngsters the use of drugs for the sake of their harmful effects was often also associated with the use of LSD or barbiturates. With adult marijuana users the drug, despite its harmful psychological consequences, did not seem to be used in the overtly self-destructive way that it commonly was with adolescents. Some of the adults we studied had used other drugs, such as heroin in earlier, more self-destructive periods of their lives.

The use of marijuana by our adolescent subjects to diminish an overwhelming or otherwise uncontrollabe anger was reflected quite differently in our adult subjects. Some who functioned effectively and competitively at work saw marijuana as necessary to reduce their competitive aggression when they were away from work sufficiently to enable them to relax. Some were threatened by competitiveness and aggression to such an extent that they smoked during the day to avoid having to deal with such feelings. If they did not use marijuana to deal with acute overwhelming anger, as our adolescent subjects did, most used it to ease the chronic anger and frustration produced by unhappy relationships.

Some of the male subjects, like Michael Forenzo, used marijuana to help sustain grandiose fantasies of success and achievement in ways that our adolescent drug abusers had. Although he occupied himself with writing and directing, his grandiosity made it difficult for him to work in any way that would be remunerative. He had the adolescent's difficulty of reconciling fantasies and possibilities.

Among most of the male subjects the transformation in mood produced by the use of marijuana was associated with grandiosity in subtler ways. For example, Daniel Pollock's sense of himself as a "philosopher-king" who had profound insights into other people while he was smoking had to be seen in the context of his remarkable need to avoid any insights into himself. Jeffrey Gordon pictured himself as a Saint Bernard dog who could survive and endure all hardships. His life had been a series of painful frustrations, and he used marijuana to avoid facing the fact that he had paid a price for not attempting to deal with them.

The illusion of invulnerability was a more common feature among women who used marijuana regularly. The adolescent girls we studied believed that there would not be harmful consequences from their destructive behavior or from relationships that were destructive to them. Many of the adult women marijuana users had continued such behavior and relationships, together with an illusion of such invulnerability, into their thirties.

Adolescents, including adolescent marijuana users, are often changing too rapidly to allow more than tentative conclusions about their future lives. The adult marijuana users had lived long enough for the patterns of their work and personal relationships and the role that marijuana played in them to become established.

None of the high school students we saw and few of the college students who were heavy users of marijuana were able to combine such usage with academic or work success. Most were deeply involved in conflicts with their families that had so negatively permeated their attitudes toward ambition and achievement as to make them intolerable or impossible goals.

By contrast, daily heavy marijuana usage was compatible with significant career success in several of the adult cases. Daniel Pollock, a lawyer, and Ellen Thornton, a writer, were good examples. Both came from ambitious and successful families; both had incorporated parental goals for achievement even though they diverged from parental values in other respects. It is significant that Daniel and Ellen conscientiously avoided smoking marijuana during the working day. Both made a careful split between their working personae and their social selves and felt marijuana was an integral part of their ability to relax.

It may be significant that both started their heavy marijuana usage in adult life: in Daniel's case, after he was in legal practice; in Ellen's, after she had been teaching, had divorced, and was living independently. Jeffrey Gordon, who had passively resigned himself to not moving ahead in his work and used marijuana both to reinforce his behavior and as a consolation, had started to smoke heavily at seventeen. At the age of thirty-five, Jeffrey still bore a strong resemblance to the adolescent marijuana abusers.

All of the heavy marijuana users we studied from the high school and college age groups had problems with intimacy. Because such problems are so common in adolescents and because their use of marijuana did not seem to play a significant role in their avoidance of closeness (in the way that heroin use clearly did), we did not consider the keeping of emotional distance a primary function of marijuana for these youngsters.

Problems in close relationships were present in virtually all of the adult daily users of marijuana, and in this group marijuana reinforced detachment and appeared to make some relationships possible and tolerable. Some, like Irene Rousseau, used marijuana to avoid facing frustration with a marital partner. Others, like Emily Leone, Michael Forenzo, and Daniel Pollock, used marijuana in the service of their sexual fantasies and behavior involving more than one partner, fantasies and behavior that clearly restricted the closeness of their primary relationship. In some casses, where the individual had established a relationship in which limited involvement was part of the relationship, as in the case of Ellen Thornton or Daniel Pollock where no young children were involved, marijuana usage seemed to become less necessary. In both of these cases the need for marijuana seemed likely to increase if the barriers to intimacy were further reduced.

AN ASSESSMENT OF MULTIPLE METHODS OF DATA COLLECTION

Throughout this investigation one of our primary interests was in comparing, contrasting, and evaluating the information we obtained from the various methods incorporated into the study: the screening session and written questionnaire, the series of interviews, and the battery of psychological tests. Our previous work with adolescents had established the effectiveness of psychodynamic interviewing in uncovering the functions and consequences of long-term, heavy drug use. The present study, which built in multiple methods of data collection, made possible a much more direct comparison between what can be learned through that approach as opposed to the written questionnaire, which has been more widely used in drug-related research.

Overall, we were favorably impressed with the forthrightness and openness that the study participants displayed in completing the questionnaire and, with few exceptions, we uncovered no evidence that they were intentionally concealing or misrepresenting their drug behavior or related aspects of their lives. Their written questionnaire responses reflected a high degree of internal consistency and were generally highly consistent as well with what had been learned about the individual from the application form, the initial telephone conversation, and the brief face-to-face interview that took place at the beginning of the screening session.

The quality of the information obtained through the questionnaires appeared to be in part a function of the personal contact that was established with the participants, which allowed them the opportunity to "feel out" the researchers and to judge for themselves the intentions and risks of the study. It also appeared likely that the interest the interviewers evidenced in the screening session in the individual participant as a unique and valued source of information and the absence of any impression of judgment encouraged openness among the subjects, as did the possibility of extended participation in the follow-up study.

Although we felt the information we obtained accurately reflected the respondents' perceptions of their behavior and feelings in almost all cases, there were several areas in which the questionnaire findings contrasted rather sharply with what was learned through the subsequent interviews and psychological tests. Perhaps the most basic of these concerned the reasons for these individuals' heavy, long-term use of marijuana. With the functions of marijuana revealed in the interviews as a background, it is worthwhile to look again at the reasons the subjects initially gave us as to the role of marijuana in their lives.

On the questionnaire more than 95 percent of the sample of 150 indicated a desire to get pleasure, to feel good, to get high, and to relax and relieve tension as reasons for their smoking marijuana. Through our intensive study of the 15 selected cases we saw how hard pleasure came to them, how seldom they felt good, how often they felt low rather than high, how tense they were, and how difficult it was for them to relax.

Those who functioned effectively and responsibly at work seemed to see the achieving, competitive responsible side of their personality as a constraint against which they struggled. They needed marijuana to put aside aspects of their personality that they could not integrate or reconcile with enjoyment.

Close personal relations with the opposite sex were also seen to be a source of tension to both men and women. Sixty percent of those completing the questionnaire indicated greater enjoyment of sex and greater sexual freedom as benefits of their marijuana smoking. Our in-depth interviews made clear the difficulties in intimacy faced by our subjects and the role of marijuana in inducing the detachment they needed for pleasurable sexual relations.

If the subjects had problems with closeness to others, most could not tolerate being alone. Daniel Pollock connected being alone with a heightened consciousness of what death must be like; and if his imagery was particularly strong, it was consistent with feelings shared by other subjects. A preoccupation with fears of death, with which some of the subjects attempted to cope through belief in reincarnation, seemed related to an already present emotional constriction and deadness that left them without emotional resources to be alone. When alone they needed to smoke; best of all, they could smoke with friends and use marijuana's effects to avoid both aloneness and intimacy. That 88 percent of the 150 subjects gave the desire to enjoy the effects of marijuana with friends as a reason for their smoking seems understandable in this context, as is the fact that 60 percent of the total group saw marijuana as helping them to overcome boredom. The interviews served to illuminate the relationship between the subjects' difficulties with closeness, emotional constriction, and the need for sensory experience with drugs or sex to make them feel alive.

Half of the subjects indicated in their questionnaire responses that they valued marijuana for its ability to help them avoid feeling depressed, and more than half indicated that it helped them to avoid anger. Intensive work with the 15 cases indicated that anger and depression were natural consequences of frustrating life situations that the subjects avoided recognizing or dealing with by repressing the emotions that signaled their discomfort.

More than 40 percent of the subjects felt marijuana improved their ability to be tolerant of other people. Early in their interviews the mothers among our selected cases particularly emphasized the effect of marijuana in making them more patient and tolerant with their children. Only as the interviews progressed did it become evident that their tolerant, "nothing bothers me" attitude derived from a detachment or "spaciness" to which their children strongly objected.

The material elicited in the interviews, although not usually directly contradicting the questionnaire responses regarding the motivations and effects of marijuana use, placed them in a context that they otherwise lacked. Yet the questionnaire data complemented the interview material, and the combination of both provided a perspective that otherwise would have been lacking. It is not simply that the questionnaire data provide guidelines as to areas worth exploring; they also provided a picture of the way in which the subjects presented themselves. The contrast between that presentation and the material revealed in the interviews was more valuable than either set of data would have been alone.

In areas of their lives not directly involving marijuana use, the data from the interviews also served to complement and deepen the information obtained from other sources. For example, our study appeared to confirm something that McGlothlin and his colleagues had found in their work with adult marijuana smokers (McGlothlin, Arnold, & Rowan, 1970): that this particular population is characterized by a higher than usual belief in such paranormal phenomena as astrology. Our interviews with the selected cases revealed that such belief could be understood in the context of the reluctance of such subjects to avoid personal responsibility for their own destinies by not looking at the role their own characters played in their problems. Similarly, the belief in reincarnation that these individuals frequently expressed reflected their wish that frustrations in their lives could be resolved in a subsequent life.

The individuals we interviewed provided considerable evidence that their questionnaire responses were often expressing only a one-dimensional glimpse of what was really going on in their lives. Rather than being true indications of high levels of life satisfaction, for example, the high scores they consistently gave to the many scaled questionnaire items on this topic appeared more often to reflect a desire not to confront those aspects of their lives that were sources of frustration or sadness. Similarly, most subjects' minimizing or outright denial on the questionnaire of the things in their lives about which they were truly troubled was in sharp contrast to the level of turmoil that was uncovered during the interviews with each of the 15 cases. Interestingly, on the questionnaire itself responses to the open-ended items dealing with past and current difficulties, particularly with families, served to modify earlier forced-choice responses on this topic and provided a better indication of the type of psychological problems that many of these men and women evidenced during the interviews.

Since there was often such a discrepancy between the information obtained on the questionnaire and that which emerged in the interviews, the high level of agreement between the psychological test results and the interviews strengthened our confidence in the clinical findings. Even more important, they added further perspective to both our understanding of the subjects' underlying self-perceptions and conflicts and the ways in which they defended themselves.

The results of the MMPI were consistent overall with the conclusions reached through the clinical interviews, to an extent that probably would not warrant the use of this time-consuming measure in conjunction with the interview procedure. At the same time, the MMPI findings added a valuable dimension to the picture of the cases that emered solely through their questionnaire responses.

Particularly striking was the fact that in almost every case the MMPI results pointed to the individual's need to deny problems and to present himself in the most favorable light. The only exception to this among the cases we have discussed here was Jeffrey Gordon, whose self-defeating and self-punitive tendencies were reflected in his questionnaire responses as well as in his MMPI. In addition, the MMPI, in identifying such problems as Ellen Thornton's difficulties in expressing hostility and in establishing relationships, or the possibility in Michael Forenzo's case of a psychotic or prepsychotic condition, provided information that although evident in these individuals' interviews was not revealed at all in their questionnaires.

The sharp contrast we found between the results of the MMPI and the questionnaire data was even more pronounced with reference to the responses on the Rorschach and Draw-A-Person Tests. In almost every case these tests uncovered a level of psychological difficulty that, if not altogether missing in the individual's questionnaire responses, was significantly underreflected.

For example, the poor form level and lack of emotional control in Michael Forenzo's Rorschach responses, and the fragility of ego boundaries suggested by the failure of his drawings to separate clearly figure and background, pointed to the nature and degree of a disturbed adaptation indicated in his interviews but not revealed in his questionnaire responses.

The psychological testing strongly reflected the tendencies of our subjcts to avoid looking at problems and to deal with them by denial. Daniel Pollock, for example, drew a happy smiling stick figure and told a story that revealed as little as possible of himself. While presenting himself as carefree, like the character in his story, his Rorschach protocol made evident the anxiety and disturbed self-image that the story attempted to conceal.

Some of the subjects were less well defended. Jeffrey Gordon's drawing and story of a cab driver drifting aimlessly through life appeared to be a clear reflection of his own sense of drifting. Similarly, Michael Forenzo directly identified with the disturbed, sexually maladjusted piano player who, according to Michael's story, ends up killing a woman.

The psychological tests revealed the difficulties with intimacy of all of our subjects. For example, Emily Leone feared being entrapped or engulfed in any close relationship. Her recurrent imagery in the Rorschach of creatures with grippers or tentacles wrapping around or devouring innocent defenseless victims was a graphic confirmation of these fears.

The Rorschach responses reflected the damaged self-image of virtually all of our subjects despite questionnaire statements that often reflected self-satisfaction. Although there was evidence of such problems in the interviews, the power of the imagery of their Rorschach responses could have been matched only by the dreams of these subjects had they been in extended psychotherapy.

The first card in the Rorschach often elicits self-image responses in the way in which the commonly seen bat or butterfly are portrayed. In all six of the cases we have presented the figure was seen as damaged or unattractive. Emily Leone's butterfly had wings that were torn and ragged. Ellen Thornton's bat had "a ghoulish face with holes in its wings." Irene Rousseau saw a hairy gypsy moth with deformed wings. Jeffrey Gordon's bat had misshapen uneven claws and torn wings. Michael Forenzo's bat had an eye missing, which he followed with a response of "an alien creature with a split head." Daniel Pollock saw "a moth trying to become a butterfly, with a head of a frog, possessing great wings too burdensome for the body, too bulky to be moving." His response suggested not only his damaged self-image but the burden of the effort to transform it.

The psychological tests also were valuable in providing confirmation of early damage and disturbance in the lives of the individuals and evidence that their experiences were still profoundly affecting them. For most of the cases, both a damaged self-image and anxiety over their needs for affection were evidenced in their Rorschach protocols. These frequently appeared to be related to frustrated needs for maternal care, as in Jeffrey Gordon's perception of a bat injured in a fight over food and Irene Rousseau's images of birth, feeding, and the newborn.

Finally, there were certain types of information that although consistent with the interviews were available only through the psychological testing. For example, although Daniel Pollock had succeeded in the business aspects of legal practice, he had long given up reading or thinking about legal problems. He paid the price for his 20 years of heavy marijuana usage in the deterioration of his intellectual functioning that was reflected in the psychological testing.

Having identified the functions marijuana was found to play in the lives of the adults whom we studied and having elaborated these in a discussion of the different perspectives that emerged through the use of multiple methods of data collection, a few concluding observations about the role of daily use of marijuana in the psychosocial adaptation of adults seem warranted. On the basis of our study marijuana is not simply a drug of passivity, withdrawal, and denial. For almost all of our subjects its use was associated with a sense of magical transformation—the transformation from frustrated wife to science fiction adventuress, from irritable mother fearing commitment to husband and children to the holder of fantasy tickets to sexual adventure, from responsible adult to playful child, from driven lawyer to "philosopher-king," and from unsuccessful screenwriter unable to support his family to talented director for whom his family's needs must be sacrificed. Following her first session, one woman dreamed that she was dead and was being led into a new life by Mr. Rourke from the TV program, *Fantasy Island*, whom she described as a "godlike individual." Her association made clear that the dream was stimulated by her hope that some such change would take place through the interviews.

Some of these men and women had achieved significant success and recognition but had ambitions that were larger and deeper than any degree of actual success was likely to satisfy. Daniel Pollock's desire to be a philosopher-king, with its connotations of an idealized classical world of thought in which one has power, genius, and perfection of character, reflected the wish to transcend life in its present terms. His response to Card 1 of the Rorschach of a moth trying to become a butterfly reflected the dark side of such extraordinary ambition in attributing to the moth the ugly face of a frog and wings so large that they were useless. The frog-moth hybrid, like the beasts of antiquity, appeared to have the desire for flight but no capacity for it. As a metaphor for this individual's condition, the response revealed considerable frustration. Marijuana was an essential part of Daniel's attempt to reduce the frustration inherent in who he was.

Among the individuals we interviewed we consistently observed their substitution of a sensory illusion of life for the boredom and fear of lifelessness that afflicted them. Such magical transformation became for many a substitute for the effort to real change. The belief in a fate dictated by the stars was consistent with the use of marijuana to change one's fate in fantasy rather than reality. For some, like Michael Forenzo, the escape was total. Others, like Daniel Pollock or Ellen Thornton, accomplished much at work and did not smoke while working; but they, like Jeffrey Gordon, Irene Rousseau, and Emily Leone, used marijuana most other times to avoid seeing, understanding, or dealing with their personal situations.

Daily heavy marijuana use for each of these adults was intimately bound up with adaptive difficulties in personal relationships and/or work and with their attempts to deal with these difficulties. We found this to be as true for subjects who presented their lives as evidence of the harmless or even beneficial consequences of smoking as it was for those who, while not blaming their smoking, were somewhat more dissatisfied with their lives.

To the degree that the subjects were aware of their difficulties, they saw marijuana as an escape from them as providing relief, or as enhancing their ability to cope with them. They did not consider marijuana to be the cause of their difficulties, and our observations did not contradict this view.

In making any judgment about the role of marijuana in the lives of daily adult users, one must raise the question of how they would manage without it. If one concludes that these individuals would not have solved their difficulties in any case, marijuana can be seen as a tranquilizer in a disturbed life. In the case of those whose anxiety and fragmentation were extremely severe, the use of marijuana to reduce anxiety and to provide focus appeared necessary to enable them to function in any adaptive way.

On the other hand, many of the men and women we studied seemed to have the potential to resolve their problems with pychotherapeutic help. In a sense, marijuana helped such individuals to avoid the discomfort that might have motivated them to seek help. In saying this, however, it also must be recognized that avoiding looking at themselves and their problems was bound up with their desire for marijuana in the first place.

The ambivalence with which many in the group approached this issue was suggested by their involvement in the interviews and their feeling that they benefited from them. Yet if they were not unalterably opposed to looking at their lives, they were prone to looking at them in selective ways. What drew them to the study appeared to be, in part, their tendency to see all activity as an "experience," and this particular experience as one that held out the possibility of transformation. Whatever hopes they had for change in their lives, however, were doomed in the context of their chronic use of marijuana. In sustaining the illusion of change and in soothing their frustration and anger at the lives they led, marijuana also was keeping them cemented in their current adaptation.

Marijuana maintained these individuals in a troubled adaptation, reinforcing their tendency not to look at, understand, or attempt to master their difficulties. It served to detach them from their problems and allowed them to regard even serious difficulties as unimportant. Marijuana provided a buffer zone of sensation that functioned as a barrier against self-awareness and closeness to others.

RORSCHACH TEST SCORES

Daniel Pollock

Location		Determinant		Content		High Significance
W	10	M	2	H	2	$W > 2M$
D	9	FM	4(1)	(H)	1	$FC' + C'F + C > 3$
d	1	FK	(2)	Hd	1	
S	(1)	F	2	A	9	
		Fc	(1)	P	5	
		FC'+	7(4)			
		FC	4(1)			
		C	1			

Emily Leone

Location		Determinant		Content		High Significance
W	8	M	6(2)	H	6	$FC' + C'F + C' > 3$
Wx	3	FM+	9	Hd	4	$FK + Fc > 75\% \ OF \ F$
D	11	m	(1)	A	9	$Fc + c + C' > 2(FC + CF + C)$
d	5	FK	2	Ad	1	
		F	1	P	4	
		Fc	1(6)	O	2	
		FC'+	8(9)			
		FC	(2)			
		CF	(1)			
		C	(1)			

Jeffrey Gordon

Location		Determinant		Content		High Significance
W	9	M	2	H	2	W>2M
D	9	FM +	9	Hd	1	FK + Fc > 75% OF F
		Fm	(1)	A	8	
		KF	1	Ad	2	
		FK	(2)	P	6	
		F	1	O	1	
		Fc	1(4)			
		FC′	1(6)			
		C′F	1			
		FC	1(2)			
		C −	1			

Ellen Thornton

Location		Determinant		Content		High Significance
W	14	M +	6(1)	H	7	W > AVE
D	3	FM	4(1)	(H)	1	D < AVE
S	(2)	m	(1)	A	3	
		F	3	P	3	
		Fc	(6)			
		FC′	4(2)			
		FC	(3)			
		CF	(1)			
		C	(3)			

Michael Forenzo

Location		Determinant		Content		High Significance
W	9	M	3(1)	H	1	FC′ + C′F + C′ > 3
Wx	1	FM	5(1)	(H)	3	CF + C > O AND C′ = 0
D	24	m −	1(1)	Hd	4	C > O
d	3	FK	1(3)	A	9	Fc > AVE
dd	4	F	8	Ad	1	FK + Fc > 75% OF F
S	(4)	Fc	7(3)	P	8	
		cF	(1)			
		FC′ −	10(4)			
		C′F	1			
		FC −	2(1)			
		C −	3(2)			

Irene Rousseau

Location		Determinant		Content		High Significance
W	15	M	3(3)	H	4	W > AVE
D	4	FM	5(1)	(H)	2	FC' + C'F + C > 3
S	1(1)	m	(2)	A	4	FK + Fc > 75% OF F
		FK	1(1)	Ad	1	CF + C > 0 AND C ' = O
		F	3	P	3	
		Fc	(6)	O	1	
		cF	(1)			
		c	(1)			
		FC'	3(7)			
		FC	3(3)			
		CF	1			
		C	1(2)			

REFERENCES

Allen, T. R., & West, L. J. (1968). Flight from violence: Hippies and the green rebellion. *American Journal of Psychiatry, 124,* 364–370.

American Psychiatric Association. (1980). *Diagnostic and statistical manual of mental disorders* (3rd. ed.). Washington, DC.

Carr, A. C. (1972). A self-report questionnaire. *Journal of Personality Assessment, 36,* 525–533.

Carr, A. C. (1980). Psychological testing of personality. In H. Kaplan, A. M. Freedman, & B. J. Sadock (Eds.), *Comprehensive textbook of psychiatry.* (pp. 940–966). Baltimore: Williams and Wilkins.

Carr, A. C. (1984). Psychological tests. In M. H. Sacks, W. H. Sledge, & M. Rubinton (Eds.), *Case readings in psychiatry* (pp. 243–252). New York: Praeger.

Castaneda, C. (1973). *The teachings of Don Juan: A Yaqui way of knowledge.* New York: Simon & Schuster.

Clayton, R., & Ritter, C. (1985). The epidemiology of alcohol and drug abuse among adolescents. *Anvances in Alcohol and Substance Abuse, 4*(3–4), 69–97.

Esman, A. H. (1967). Drug use by adolescents: Some valuative and technical implications. *Psychoanalytic Forum, 2,* 340–353.

Grinspoon, L. (1971). *Marijuana reconsidered.* Cambridge, MA: Harvard University Press.

Halikas, J. A., Weller, R. A., Morse, C. L., & Hoffman, R. G. (1983). Regular marijuana use and its effect on psychosocial variables: A longitudinal study. *Comprehensive Psychiatry, 24,* 229–235.

Hammer, E. (1980). *The clinical application of projective drawings.* Springfield, IL: Charles C. Thomas.

Hendin, H. Marijuana abuse among college students. (1973). *Journal of Nervous and Mental Disease, 156,* 259–270.

Hendin, H. (1975). *The age of sensation.* New York: W. W. Norton.

Hendin, H. (1980). Psychosocial theory of drug abuse: A psychodynamic approach. In D. J. Lettieri, M. Sayers, & H. W. Pearson, (Eds.), *Theories on drug abuse: Selected contemporary perspectives* (pp. 195–200). National Institute on Drug Abuse Research Monograph 30. DDHS Pub. No. (ADM) 80-967. Washington, DC: U.S. Government Printing Offices.

Hendin, H., Pollinger, A., Ulman, R., & Carr, A. (1981). *Adolescent marijuana abusers and their families.* National Institute on Drug Abuse Research Monograph 40. DDHS Pub. No. (ADM) 81-1168. Washington, DC: U.S. Government Printing Offices.

Hochman, J. S., & Brill, N. G. (1973). Chronic marijuana use and psychosocial adaptation. *American Journal of Psychiatry, 130,* 132–140.

Huba, G., Bentler, P., & Newcomb, M. (1981). *Assessing marijuana consequences: Selected questionnaire items.* National Institute on Drug Abuse Research Issues 28. DDHS Pub. No. (ADM) 81-1150. Washington, DC: U.S. Government Printing Office.

Jessor, R. (1976). Predicting time of onset of marijuana use: A developmental study of high school youth. *Journal of Consulting and Clinical Psychology, 44,* 25–34.

Jessor, R. (1979): Marijuana: A review of recent psychosocial research. In: R. I. Dupont, J. Goldstein, V. A. O'Donnell, & B. Brown (Eds.), *Handbook of drug abuse* (pp. 337–355). Washington, DC: U.S. Government Printing Office.

Jessor, R., Chase, J. A., & Donovan, S. E. (1980). Psychosocial correlates of marijuana and problem drinking in a national sample of adolescents. *American Journal of Public Health, 70,* 604–613.

Jessor, R., & Jessor, S. L. (1977). *Problem behavior and psychosocial development: A longitudinal study of youth.* New York: Academic Press.

Jessor, R., Jessor, S. L., & Finney, J. A. (1973). Social psychology of marijuana use: Longitudinal studies of high school and college youth. *Journal of Personality and Social Psychology, 26,* 1–15.

Kandel, D. B. (1973) The role of parents and peers in adolescent marijuana use. *Science, 181,* 1067–1070.

Kandel, D. B., Kessler, R. C., & Margulies, R. Z. (1978). Antecedents of adolescent initiation into stages of drug use: A developmental analysis. In D. B. Kandel (Ed.), *Longitudinal research on drug use: Empirical findings and methodological issues.* New York: John Wiley & Sons.

Kaplan, H. B. (1975a). Increase in self-rejection as an antecedent of deviant response. *Journal of Youth and Adolesence, 4,* 281–292.

Kaplan, H. B. (1975b). The self-esteem motive and change in self-attitudes. *Journal of Nervous and Mental Disease, 161,* 265–275.

Kaplan, H. B. (1978). Deviant behavior and self-enhancement in adolescence. *Journal of Youth and Adolesence, 7,* 253–277.

Knight, R. G. (1983). On intepreting the several standard errors of the WAIS-R: Some further tables. *Journal of Consulting and Clinical Psychology, 51,* 671–673.

Kolansky, H., & Moore, W. T. (1971). Effects of marijuana on adolescents and young adults. *Journal of the American Medical Association, 216,* 486–492.

Kolansky, H., & Moore, W. T. (1972). Toxic effects of chronic marijuana use. *Journal of the American Medical Association, 222,* 34–41.

Kolodny, R. C., Masters, W. H., Kolodner, R. M., & Toro, E. (1974). Depression of plasma testosterone levels after chronic intensive marijuana use. *New England Journal of Medicine, 290,* 872–874.

Kornhaber, A. (1971). Marijuana in an adolescent psychiatric outpatient population. *Journal of the American Medical Association, 215,* 1988.

Kupfer, D. J., Detre, T., Korall, J., & Fajans, P. (1973). A comment on the "amotivational syndrome" in marijuana smokers. *American Journal of Psychiatry, 130,* 1319–1322.

Maugh, T. H. (1974). Marijuana. II. Does it damage the brain? *Science, 185,* 775–776.

McGlothlin, W. H., Arnold, D., & Rowan, P. (1970) Marijuana use among adults. *Psychiatry, 33,* 433–443.

McGlothlin, W. H., & West, L. J. (1968). The marijuana problem: An overview. *American Journal of Psychiatry, 125:* 370–278.

Miller, J., & Cissin, I. (1983). *Highlights from the National Survey on Drug Abuse: 1982.* Washington, DC: U.S. Government Printing Office.

Mirin, S. M., Shapiro, L. M., Meyer, R. E., Pillard, R. C., & Fisher, S.

(1971). Casual versus heavy use of marijuana: A redefinition of the marijuana problem. *American Journal of Psychiatry, 127,* 1134–1140.

Naglieri, J. A. (1982). Two types of tables for use with the WAIS-R. *Journal of Consulting and Clinical Psychology, 50,* 319–321.

Norem-Hebeisen, A. A. (1975). Self-esteem as a predictor of adolescent drug abuse. In D. J. Lettieri (Ed.), *Predicting adolescent drug abuse: A Review of issues, methods and correlates* (pp. 193–206). National Institute on Drug Abuse Research Issue Series 11. DHEW Pub. No. (ADM) 76-299. Washington, DC: U.S. Government Printing Office.

Petersen, R. C. (1980). Marijuana and health: 1980. In R. C. Petersen (Ed.), *Marijuana research findings: 1980.* (pp. 1–53). National Institute on Drug Abuse Research Monograph 31. DHHS Pub. No. (ADM) 80-1001. Washington, DC: U.S. Government Printing Offices.

Richards, L. G. (1981). *Demographic trends and drug abuse, 1980–1995.* National Institute on Drug Abuse Research Monograph 35. DHHS Pub. No. (ADM) 81-1069. Washington, DC: U.S. Government Printing Office.

Robins, L., Darvish, H., & Murphy, G. (1970). The long-term outcome for adolescent drug users: A follow-up study of 76 users and 146 nonusers. In J. Zubin & A. Freedman (Eds.), *The psychopathology of adolescence* (pp. 159–178). New York: Grune and Stratton.

Winick, C. (1970). The use of drugs by jazz musicians. *Social Problems, 7,* 240–253.

INDEX